The Promise

By Mary Teegardin
Edited by M E Tewksbury

Illustrated by the Author
Cover Illustration by Drew Thurston

© OMF INTERNATIONAL
(formerly China Inland Mission)

Published by Overseas Missionary Fellowship (USA) Ltd.
10 W. Dry Creek Circle, Littleton, CO 80120-4413

Published 2003

ISBN 1-929122-16-0
Reading level: Grade 6.5   Interest level: Age 12 and up

Additional illustrations by the Lammermuir Community

All rights reserved, including translation. No part of this book may be reproduced or transmitted in any form or by any means, electronic or mechanical, including photocopying, recording, or any information storage and retrieval system without written permission from OMF International, 2 Cluny Road, Singapore 259570, Republic of Singapore. Printed in the United States of America.

OMF Books are distributed by
OMF, 10 West Dry Creek Circle, Littleton, CO 80120, USA
OMF, Station Approach, Borough Green, Sevenoaks, Kent TN15 8BG, United Kingdom
OMF, PO Box 849, Epping, NSW 2121, Australia
OMF, 5155 Spectrum Way, Bldg 21, Mississauga, ON L4W 5A1, Canada
OMF, PO Box 10159, Auckland, New Zealand
OMF, PO Box 3080, Pinegowrie 2123, South Africa
and other OMF offices.

Table of Contents

1	Kindness and Creepy Crawlies	7
2	Hints of the Future	11
3	Discovery in the Woods	15
4	I Make a Promise	19
5	Mother Remembers	23
6	Opposition	25
7	Guidance	29
8	Westward to the East	33
9	China!	37
10	So Much to Learn	41
11	God Gets My Attention	45
12	The "Thanksgiving Key"	49
13	When the Key Doesn't Turn	53
14	Teacher Ho	57
15	The Threat of War	63
16	A Visit to Tribal Land	67
17	Tribal Hospitality	71
18	Ministry in the Valley	77
19	As the Storm Gathers	83
20	Liberation	85
21	"Liberties"	89
22	Harassed!	93
23	Imprisonment and Provision	97
24	Crucible of Fear	101
25	Despair	105
26	Surprises in the Attic	109
27	Christmas Comes Late	115
28	Testing	119
29	Ostracized	123

30	Perfect Timing	127
31	Help With Our Packing?	131
32	Last Preparations	135
33	Caught with Contraband	137
34	At the Police Station	143
35	Good-bye to Luhsien	147
36	Road to Freedom	151
37	Stopped at the Border!	155

China

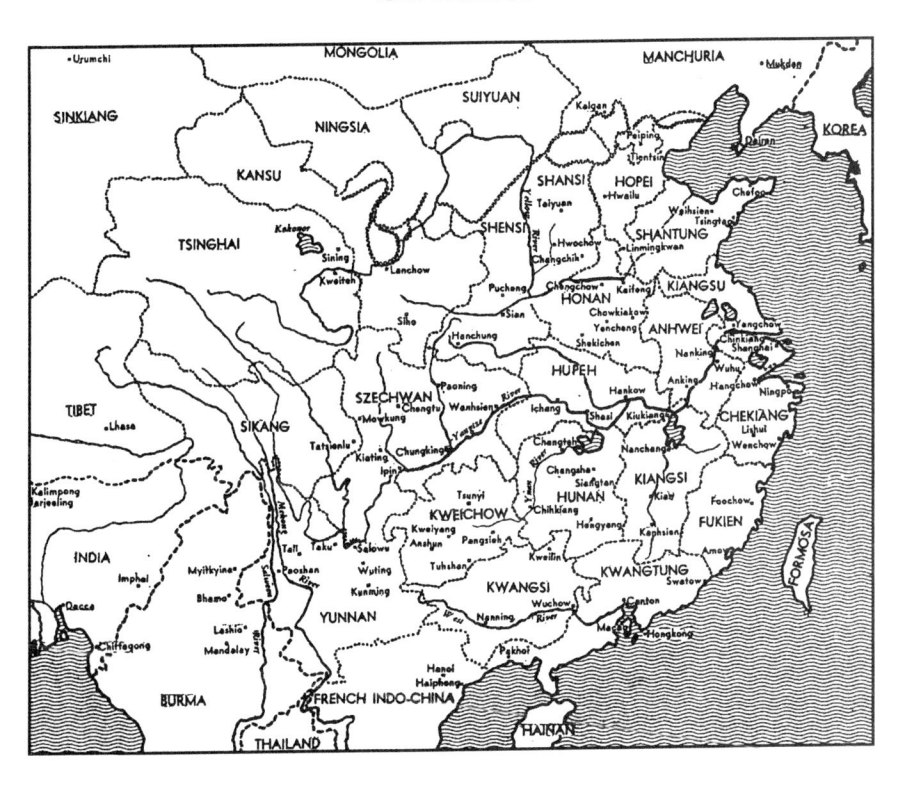

Chapter One

Kindness and Creepy-Crawlies

M"ary," Mother called from the kitchen, "go to the chicken coop and get me some eggs. I want to make gingerbread for supper."

I plunked down the giant headphones of my father's crystal-radio set. I tugged on my jacket and ran out into the blustery autumn air.

Chickens eyed me from wooden nests on the walls of the hen house. I tested the mood of each hen with a sleeved elbow before I slipped my hand under her breast. Finally, my pockets were filled with warm eggs. I turned to leave.

Bang! A gust of wind caught the door and blew it shut. A high, wooden latch jolted into place. I was locked in!

Would the chickens' water pail make me tall enough to reach the latch? I wondered. I tipped the water onto the floor and mounted the up-turned bucket. Still too short! But from the top of the bucket I spied rivulets of water flowing toward a tiny hatchway in the wall. A curious hen pecked at the wet litter. Then she slipped out the little door.

"Hey, I can do that," I said aloud.

"Are you coming with the eggs?" came Mother's urgent call.

I jumped from the bucket and wriggled my five-year-old body through the hatch. Standing up, I felt my pockets. *Oh no!* I did not find one whole egg!

Crushed shells oozed raw egg. It mixed with the mucky water already staining my clothes. Then through hot tears I spied an impatient figure rounding the corner of the building.

Mother stopped, gasped, then came to me. She took my slimy hand without a word of reproach. Then she led me back to the house for a warm bath. She said nothing about it at our gingerbread-less supper.

Years later, I remembered Mother's gentle example when a horrified nurse's aide in training brought me thirty-four broken thermometers. She had boiled them to sterilize them.

On hot summer days, the drone of Father's honey bees attracted me. I had been warned many times to keep away. But I still liked to creep to the base of one of those humming hives. I lay quietly with my head only inches from the entrance—listening, watching, smelling. I imagined I could see what Father had described: rows of air-conditioning bees. They took places, like soldiers, along corridors of honeycomb. To keep the wax walls from melting, they fanned their wings.

I watched worker bees spill out and fly away. Others returned from the fields, loaded with honey and pollen. They dodged past me to settle at the doors of their bustling high-rises. Housekeeper bees tumbled from the hives onto the grass, burdened with waxy debris.

Those hard-working honey makers never stung me. But later, playing somewhere far from the apiary, I stepped on a bee. It had been caught in the grass. It stung me. As I nursed a painful foot, I felt betrayed. I was also sorry for the bee. I knew it would die without a stinger.

After that, my friendship with honey bees began to decline. But I was never afraid of flying insects. This would help me cope with the scores of "creepy-crawlies" I later saw in Asia.

Chapter Two

Hints of the Future

I owe a lot to my father. He never brushed off my endless questions. And he told superb stories. Many a summer evening I lay on the cool grass near him and listened to stories while he smoked. I liked the smell of his cigars. The smoke kept mosquitoes away.

Some nights he quoted Shakespeare or long portions from Tennyson, Longfellow, or Browning. Sometimes he told tales of Roman or Greek mythology. I especially liked stories of pioneer days and American Indians.

One time we saw the northern lights flash like filmy fairies in the darkening sky. He explained what they were. He also told me about the constellations that twinkled through the pine branches above us.

Once when we were talking about the moon and the sun, I asked, "Papa, where does the sun go when it sinks behind those trees in the woods?"

His eyes squinted against the cigar smoke. He looked down at me with a hint of a smile. "To China, far away to the west. Where west becomes east. It's beginning to be day there now." He left me to puzzle over that one! Little did he know that one day I would follow that sun to China.

On long winter evenings Father usually read in an arm chair by the parlor door. Mother sat in a straight-backed rocker by the stove. She had a mending basket on her lap. My older brother, Preston, crouched over the radio. From that mysterious box, he coaxed crackling sounds, voices, or music. Ruth and Orville, busy with homework, sat at the library table near a kerosene lamp.

Helen and I were the youngest. We dressed and undressed our dolls. Or we dressed the kittens we took from a box behind the stove.

Sometimes we grew tired of play. "Mama, what can we do now?" we asked.

Laying down the heavy sock she darned, Mother would suggest a game. "What about 'hide the thimble'?"

We would dance impatiently while she searched her basket for a spare thimble. We loved the game.

The familiar old living room held lots of shadowy places to hide the thimble. Shrieks of delight shattered the peace each time one of us found the hidden treasure. But when the clock on the high mantel stroked eight, we knew our game was over. "Bedtime," Mother called.

Reluctantly we dressed in our night clothes. We dallied until a curt "Hike!" came from Father.

Warm blankets hung from the backs of chairs near the stove. Wrapping them around us, we said goodnight. We scampered to our cold bedroom as quickly as the blankets allowed. As we climbed into bed, our fingers groped for warm bricks, wrapped in newspaper. Mother had put them there earlier. We pulled them to our feet and soon fell fast asleep.

We were never kissed or tucked in, but we felt secure and loved. Years later, I noticed a similar lack of outward affection in oriental homes. I knew it didn't mean there was no love there.

On gusty winter days I preferred to play in the parlor. It was out of bounds without Mother there. She would play the organ or work on a quilt.

I never tired of looking at pictures. I found them in a red velvet album or stashed in the lower drawer of Mother's desk. Through those pictures I looked back into family history.

In one faded picture, a bearded farmer wore homemade, high-top leather boots. He was Grandfather Teegardin. A scratched tintype of a young surveyor introduced me to Grandfather Morley.

I studied one photo endlessly. It showed Grandfather and Grandmother Teegardin. It was their golden wedding anniversary in 1911. They sat at a table reading a Bible. I often wondered what was in the book that gave them such peaceful expressions. I never asked. Our family seldom talked about religion.

From other photos, Mother told how Grandpa Metz came to live in her home when her mother remarried. Mother's own father died when she was eight. Grandpa Metz was the only grandparent I ever really knew.

Mother also told me how Papa had to withdraw from the college where they met. His father was ill. After the first year of college, he went home to manage the family farm. My parents didn't marry until after Mother had taught school for several years.

At the bottom of the drawer lay a large family photo. It had been taken when I was four. Mother did not like that picture. She usually hurried to put it away. "I look sick," she said.

Mother *was* ill. She had begun her long struggle with tuberculosis. I don't remember when I began to understand why she boiled her dishes after each meal. God used her carefulness to protect my life for His purpose.

Chapter Three

Discovery in the Woods

*I*n my fourth year at school, they combined the town's one-room schools. The changes disturbed me. I lost confidence and became discouraged and defensive.

It was hard to make new friends. I had no one to share my feelings with, so I yearned for God. But I didn't know how to find Him. The stories we heard in Sunday school didn't seem to have anything to do with me.

My parents had been active in church after they were first married. They kept Sunday as a day of rest, but by the time I was born they rarely went to Sunday services. We did not hear the Bible read aloud in our home. We heard prayers spoken only before meals or when Grandpa Metz came. We learned morals more by example than by words.

Deep inside I knew I fell short of the standards. The emptiness in my heart deepened. Then an embarrassing experience pushed me to a wonderful discovery.

A new immigrant family from Hungary had moved into our community. On opening day of school, a petite, olive-skinned girl with hazel eyes came to our fifth-grade room. As our teacher introduced Rosa, she curtseyed like a princess. That lovely curtsey kept us from noticing her big, frightened eyes.

The teacher cleared his throat. "Now," he said, "Will you all please stand and say, 'Welcome to our class, Rosa.'"

Class began. During the morning I smelled an unusual odor in the room. After recess, when all windows stood open, the odor grew even stronger.

Sometime during the morning I wrote a note to a friend a few seats away. "Surely the smell comes from Rosa," I wrote. "She must be very dirty."

At noon the mystery was solved. The strange odor was garlic! The new family used it freely.

The school bell had barely stopped ringing after lunch when our teacher ordered me to the principal's office. The look on his face told me it was no ordinary errand.

Panic made my legs wooden. It grew to near terror when I saw my note on the principal's desk. Sternly, the principal read the words on that crumpled scrap of paper. He rebuked me for the mean things I had written. I knew I deserved it.

After telling me to apologize to Rosa, the principal let me go. No walk was ever so painful as my return to our classroom. Titters and knowing nudges from classmates shamed me.

I delayed my apology until after class. I flung an

"I'm sorry," toward Rosa. Then I climbed onto the waiting school bus. A glance at my older sister told me the awful news had gone ahead of me. I slumped into a seat.

Reaching home, I raced into the house. I changed out of school clothes and fled to the woods. My usual evening chore was to bring the cows from the field or woods for milking. That afternoon I first sought out a favorite hiding place.

In the far corner of Father's woods stood a maple tree. Its gnarled branches hung down, touching the grass. I had often poured out my troubles to that friendly tree. But this time I had a burden too big for a tree.

I felt wicked and alone. I left the old tree and ducked into a nearby grove of aspen. There I knelt. That spot became an altar. I confessed my terrible guilt to the God I hardly knew and felt his forgiveness flood my heart.

I went back to the old tree and flung myself on the ground, sobbing. Much later I heard my brother calling the cows. The dim, rhythmic tinkle of bells followed. Heavy with milk, the beasts plodded up the lane. As the sun sank low in the west, I got up and started home.

I could face the family now. It no longer seemed impossible to return to school the next day. Never again would I be so totally alone. I had found the "Friend that sticks closer than a brother."

Chapter Four

I Make a Promise

God used an eighth-grade assignment to help free me of insecurity. Our teacher told us to compose a "Career Book." We had to write a chapter for every career we had ever considered. Visions of homemaker, candy-store clerk, seamstress, teacher, and artist all danced before me. *Yes,* I thought, *I'll like this project.*

Then I remembered one summer evening. The memory had stayed in my heart, secret but very much alive. I wondered how I could describe it. I was afraid others would laugh if I shared it.

It troubled me for days. *Maybe I can just leave it out*, I thought. *No one will know.* But in the end I knew the last chapter of my Career Book must be titled, "Missionary."

The summer I was ten, a traveling evangelist held tent meetings about a mile from our home. Neighbors took us children to the services. I don't remember much of what the evangelist said. But I knew he had answers to questions that had troubled me a long time.

He talked about a God you could know and reach.

He was the true God. He had already reached out to us by giving His Son, Jesus Christ, to die on a cross for our sins. Not only that, Jesus had risen from the dead. And He promised to come again to take all who trust in Him to be with Him forever.

I wanted to know more. I was bitterly disappointed one evening when Father did not let me to go to the meeting. I went to my room crying. Later I heard singing and sat up to catch the distant sounds. At that moment a soft glow filtered into the room. Ever so clearly, I heard the words, "Mary, will you be a missionary for Me?"

"Yes, Lord," I whispered.

The music ceased. The glow faded.

Alarmed, I ran down the hall to my brother Orville's room.

"What's the matter?" he asked, startled.

"Did you hear anything?" I asked.

"No," he replied, yawning.

"Any music?"

"No-o-o!" he mumbled. As an afterthought he said, "Oh, maybe it was the neighbor's radio."

I did not correct him. Nor did I explain why I had come or what I had seen and heard. After a while I went back to my room, but not to sleep.

All was dark and quiet. I lay for a long time and thought about the unusual happenings. The music could have come from the tent meeting. Sounds carry far on quiet summer evenings. The light might have been a last ray of sunlight reflected off a cloud. But the voice had been so clear, so near, so real. It had to be from God.

My "yes" to that voice was the promise that set the course of my life.

When I finished my composition, I gave it to Mother for checking. The following morning I found my carefully corrected work on a stack of homework ready for school. The school bus was due. The house buzzed as Mother came in from chores. She made no comment about what I had written. Several years passed before she did.

Chapter Five

Mother Remembers

*T*he Great Depression knocked the country off its feet for nearly all of the 1930s. Just before the Wall Street crash, Father mortgaged the farm. He wanted to build a new barn and remodel our house. That mortgage put great pressure on our resources.

We all worked to save our farm from bankruptcy. I had little time or money for normal teenage pastimes.

I was not happy. I fussed about plain meals and boring school lunches. I did not appreciate the well-made dresses Mother and my sister Ruth sewed for me. Instead I longed for store-bought clothes. I begged for a new coat, though Mother's only coat was a threadbare, light-weight jacket.

In spite of my bad attitude, those years taught me lessons I would need for the future. I learned that harvest comes after long and often heart-breaking labor.

*T*he worst was over before I finished high school. I wanted to go right to further education. Father insisted his girls first get experience outside our home. My parents found a live-in job for me. It was with a family who had five small children.

The Depression had depleted Mother's strength. That autumn she entered a tuberculosis sanitarium. Rest and healthy food were the only treatments available then. It brought back some strength. But overall she continued to get worse.

The following summer, doctors allowed Mother to come home for a few weeks. I remember one special day alone with her. Not thinking of her, I tired her with my endless chit-chat. At one point, I talked about a model home I had seen. "I'd like one like that some day," I said.

Mother's response surprised me: "No, Mary, you're not going to have a house like that. You're going to have a little grass hut down in South America." It was the only time she ever hinted at what she had read in my Career Book. Three mornings later they told me she had slipped away during the night.

At nineteen I wished I had more years with Mother. But I was grateful for that last day together. It encouraged me that she remembered my promise and believed I would fulfill it.

Chapter Six

Opposition

My wise father had been right. Two years as housemaid gave me valuable experience. I learned how it felt to receive orders and correction. I also learned the importance of encouragement from an employer.

Father could not yet pay for me to study microbiology. Instead, he encouraged me to consider nursing. I applied and was accepted at the Methodist Hospital School of Nursing in Indianapolis.

During my first year there, I searched for a church that "fit." Then the pressure of work and study crowded in. I stopped looking. Sometimes, as work allowed, I joined Youth for Christ rallies and Nurses Christian Fellowship meetings.

During my second year, a friend invited me to church. It reminded me of those earlier tent meetings.

After a hearty hymn or two, the pastor called for testimonies. I began to feel uncomfortable. I was in the middle of a pew near the front. I could not escape. I tried to close my mind and ears—until the words of a young student caught my attention.

"I'm thankful to know Jesus as my personal Savior," he said. He told how God had helped him that day at school. "I'm glad I have eternal life," he ended, "and am God's child forever."

Presumption! I thought. I refused to believe it possible to have such a relationship with the God of the universe. But deep in my heart I wished for that relationship!

Some months later an upper-classman invited me to a Bible conference. I didn't know what to expect, but I agreed to go.

I learned that salvation from sin and the power to live a spiritual life does not come by "doing." It comes by trusting in what Jesus Christ has already done.

My Bible became interesting. Prayer came alive as I talked to my heavenly Father.

When Father came for my graduation, I told him I planned to get missionary training. He did not approve. He insisted I return home for a few days before doing anything else.

A stressful weekend followed. "What about your interest in microbiology?" Father asked. "That's a coming field, you know. It has a good future and money. If you will forget this idea of being a missionary, I'll put you through university. I'll pay all your fees. And you won't need to pay me back."

Father's words astounded me. I was afraid I would cry if I tried to answer so I sat quietly for a few minutes. Then I shook my head.

Again he urged me to consider his generous offer.

I stood to go. Through tears I said, "Dad, this desire to be a missionary is not something pushed on me by friends. I've known for years, even before I went into nursing."

I turned toward the stairs. Calling me back, Father reached into the magazine rack beside his chair. He pulled out two catalogs and held them out to me. "I wonder if you have considered all the options, Mary," he said quietly. On the catalog covers I saw the names, "Columbia University" and "Moody Bible Institute."

My head and my heart whirled. I took the books and climbed the steps. Sleep did not come easily that night. I realized how inconsiderate I had been in not telling Father about my missionary call earlier. He had never read my "Career Book."

The nine-mile drive back to the bus the next morning passed too quietly.

I knew I had to repay my nursing-school debt before I considered further education. Back in Indianapolis, I canceled my application to seminary. Instead, I took a job in a small county hospital. By living frugally, I was debt-free in ten months.

With State Board Exams for nursing behind me, I applied for missionary training again. A few days later, my family called me home. Father had gotten a nasty back injury in a farm accident.

One evening I took my dinner to my father's room so we could eat together. When he asked about my plans, I told him I had applied to a Bible school. This time I sensed no disapproval. "How do you plan to pay tuition and fees?" he asked.

"I will work and study at the same time," I replied.

In response Father offered to help if I needed it.

I appreciated his offer, but I felt I should refuse. I had just begun to take my first baby steps of faith. I needed to learn complete dependence on my heavenly Father.

When Dad improved, I returned to my job. Some time later, a friend and I boarded the train for Philadelphia. We were off to begin our new adventure in learning. We arrived with little money or wisdom, but a growing faith.

Chapter Seven

Guidance

Every day at the school's chapel services, speakers presented needs from around the world. *Where can I help?* I wondered as I listened.

The last year of Bible school came. I began to pray specifically: "Lord, direct me to the mission You want me to work with."

The Lord's answer came one snowy December Sunday. Several of us went to the church of one of our favorite professors. That day, three people from the China Inland Mission led the service. As they spoke, the Lord gave a quiet assurance. CIM was His choice for me.

Twelve days after I graduated from Bible school, I entered CIM's summer candidate program. Ten weeks later, as I left, I carried a thick Chinese/English dictionary with a list of the 214 radicals. In different combinations, these radicals make up all Chinese characters. We had to learn them on our voyage to China!

We also took with us an "outfit list." It listed all the things we would need for the next seven years in

China.

I took the overnight train home to Indiana. I had to be ready to sail in five weeks! And our cases and trunks had to be at the San Francisco dock a week before we sailed. That meant we had only four weeks to collect and pack for the years ahead. The days that followed were an adventure in buying, sewing, labeling, packing and freighting items from that incredible outfit list.

Most of those hectic weeks blur together. But my memory of the last Sunday at home will always remain special. Father accepted an invitation to a farewell program at the neighborhood church I had gone to as a child.

After the dinner and program, Father and I drove home. As I reached to open the car door, Father said, "Mary, there's something I want to tell you."

I waited for him to continue.

"When your mother and I were first married, before any of you children came, we pledged one of you to God for special service." With great feeling he added, "I guess you're the one."

Completely surprised, I struggled to sort out my

feelings. I remembered times I had taken offense at Father's efforts to direct me. Now I understood. What had seemed like disapproval had been his way of making me sure of the path I chose.

How strange! God's direction for my life had been set in motion long before the night I couldn't go to the tent meeting. It had been when a young bride and groom promised one of their unborn children to God for His service.

Chapter Eight

Westward to the East

*I*t was time for me to leave home for China. Father drove me quietly to the local train depot. I stopped in Colorado to see a newborn niece. My send-off from there was less subdued.

I had reservations out of Denver on the last train that could get me to the West Coast before our ship sailed. Therein lurked disaster!

On departure day, my bags were packed into my brother-in-law's car. We had just turned from the driveway when those waving good-bye shouted, "Stop! You have a flat tire!"

We quickly reloaded the baggage into a neighbor's car. Several miles later, in a residential area, the borrowed car developed a flat! My brother-in-law remembered a filling station a few blocks back and set off running. I fidgeted with my watch. He returned with the owner of the gas station. He had persuaded him to close his shop and drive us to the train station.

We frantically transferred bags. The train would leave any minute. We urged our good-hearted chauffeur to hurry, but each time he tried to go faster, the wheels of the old car shimmied.

We crept up to the cavernous train station right at departure time. We grabbed my baggage and raced toward the already-moving San Francisco Express. As the train gathered speed, I leaped from the platform onto the next-to-last coach. My breathless brother-in-law threw my heavy bags in behind me. In tears, I collapsed into an empty seat. A kind porter had witnessed our wild race. Before long, he came to show me to my berth several cars forward.

The train climbed into snow-covered mountains. Craggy peaks glowed in the setting sun. Later, they shone in brilliant moonlight. As we wound our way past them, I relaxed. For the first time in weeks, I didn't have to hurry.

The next day we sped through Utah's flat salt lands. By evening we climbed into high mountains again. *The Creator of those towering citadels loves and cares for me*, I thought.

Three days out of Denver, we rolled into California's lush valleys.

The following afternoon our group boarded the *Marine Adder*. It was a converted troop ship. We would sail nearly half way around the world in it. Our cabin had no porthole and contained four triple-deck bunks. It housed eleven of us for the next twenty-four days. For reasons soon obvious, we called our ship "The Marine Odor."

The Hawaiian Islands, then the Philippines, finally the continent of Asia seemed to rise out of the sea. Our last day at sea, we steamed into water made muddy by the Yangtze River. The sea lay glassy calm that evening, glowing in the sunset.

I stayed on deck until the coastline appeared. *What will China hold for me?* I wondered. *What will I be able to give to her? Will some of her people come to know the Savior because I have come?*

Chapter Nine

China!

Near noon the next day we docked in Shanghai's crowded port. All was confusion. Relatives welcomed thronging passengers. Coolies clamored for business.

Mission workers welcomed us like family. They shepherded us through immigration, immunizations, and customs. Finally, we gathered our hand luggage and left.

Our truck honked its way through the choked lanes and broad boulevards of Shanghai. From the back of the open vehicle, we laughed and waved to friendly pedestrians.

We spent eleven days at our mission's international headquarters in Shanghai. Mission directors interviewed us. Their wives invited us to tea. Other senior workers took us to cloth shops. There they bought plain cloth with the wildly inflated currency. We took our new fabric to tailor shops where it would be sewn into ankle-length quilted Chinese gowns.

We were eager to get to language school in Anking. But the war concerned us. Twice the office booked tickets on Yangtze River steamers for us. Twice the military commandeered the boats.

In the end we traveled by train to Nanking. It was the capital of China at that time. We had a better chance of catching a boat going upriver from there.

When we pulled out of Shanghai's central station, every car on the train seemed filled to capacity. Yet at every sub-station more people scrambled on. They were seeking safety in the countryside. Every bit of floor space filled up. We hardly had a place to put our feet! Outside the city and police control, people climbed onto the tops of the coaches. They sat on their baskets or rolled-up bedding.

Mid-afternoon we reached Nanking. We went straight to the river to find the boat booked for us.

And we thought our cabins on the ocean liner cramped! They were luxury compared to the cabin four of us now shared. It was five and a half feet square!

A stool and three bunks with bare boards were the room's only furniture. I slept on the floor. Each night I zipped my sleeping bag shut and hoped, in vain, to keep little creatures from sharing my bed! Day and night, curious Chinese peered through our two barred windows. They watched every move we made and shut out fresh air.

The first two nights our little steamer docked at cities where other missionaries lived. They invited us to their homes for evening meals. How wonderful to escape our tiny quarters for even those few hours!

That little square of space was our living room, dining room, bedroom and bathroom all in one. Each morning we received a container of wash water. Mid-morning and mid-afternoon a galley worker brought us a wooden bucket. It contained rice and a bowl of hot soup or fried vegetables.

The missionary men who escorted us slept on the crowded deck outside our door. They emptied our waste for us by throwing it overboard.

The third night we anchored midstream. The following afternoon we reached Anking.

Chinese helpers from the language school met us at the dock. They carried our bags hung from the ends of shoulder poles or in squeaking wheelbarrows. Gleeful children danced about us as we picked our way along narrow lanes. They laughed and pointed at our strange clothes, shoes, hats, hair, and noses. Finally we reached the gate of the Gospel Hall. Behind the church stood our language school.

So far, I had been able to only nod and smile—possibly at the wrong time. I was ready to tackle language learning in earnest.

Chapter Ten

So Much to Learn

School routines began at six each morning. The gardener jolted us awake by furiously beating a large brass gong. He must have smiled to himself, imagining the stir he created within!

Our days ended with the soft whir of the class buzzer at ten.

I was soon dismayed at the incredible difference between the sounds my teacher made and those coming from my mouth! I stumbled over strange grammar and script. I began to feel stupid.

After a month, the superintendent divided our class into two groups. I was in the slower group. He also urged us to guard our personal Bible study and prayer times. "Those who pray the most will get the language the quickest," he said.

I took his words seriously. I got up at five-thirty, then at five o'clock. In my dark, cold room I hurried through a sponge bath in water from my hot water bottle. After dressing in several layers of clothing, I hurried along the dark hall to the outside toilet. When I returned, mine was still the only light. *I shall do all right now*, I thought.

Bible study grew tiresome. Prayer seemed barren. I stayed near the bottom of the class.

Some weekends our mentors took us to quaint shops in the city. Or we went for walks outside the old city wall. We went in small groups to create less of a stir.

We often saw battalions of young soldiers. Some had rasping coughs. They trudged along the muddy roads with only straw sandals on their feet. Even in the damp chill, they sweated under loads of heavy equipment.

Winter winds penetrated our rooms. Stoves drove the chill from common rooms, but not from the bedrooms. Fuel oil was scarce and expensive in war-torn China. The common earthenware braziers that held live charcoal warmed our feet. They didn't warm our cold noses!

I rejoiced when spring arrived. We walked past country homes, now surrounded by flowering fruit trees. It revived my sagging spirit. Laughing children played around us as we gathered wild flowers. When they answered some of my simple questions, I exulted. *Maybe I can get this language after all!* I thought.

But back at school I wallowed in self-pity while others surged ahead.

Few of us knew what kind of work we would do—or where. My hopes and fears focused on "designation day" in April. On that day, a mission director would come for interviews and would appoint us to our new fields of service.

For months I had prayed for a new medical work. It was with an unreached people group near the border of Tibet. I hoped I would be assigned there.

I was not called until the third afternoon. The director was a saintly English gentleman named John Sinton. He had a pleasant, relaxed manner. After prayer, his first question was to the point: "Mary, how would you like to join the medical team to the Nosu people on the borders of Tibet?"

I thought my heart would burst! After my enthusiastic "I would!" we prayed together about the new work. We talked about where I could go to continue Chinese language study. I had to do this before heading to the land of the Nosu.

As my first excitement faded, gnawing fears crept in. *That will mean learning another language! Can I do that? At the rate I'm learning Chinese it will take years! I will have forgotten all of my nursing by then!*

I knew God's promises. I could not forget the promise I had made either. Still my questions remained.

I hesitated from habit. I excused myself with, *Well, I can't help it. After all, I'm only human!* I had not yet learned to submit to God's will. My defeat and frustration would continue until God got my reluctant attention.

Chapter Eleven

God Gets My Attention

Only those of us in the second stream remained at the language school. One day a message came. "Be ready to leave at a moment's notice," it said. The order did not surprise us. We could hear the rumble of distant shelling. Sometimes there was gunfire nearby. We knew our situation was dangerous.

The next morning our school exploded with activity. Carriers ferried luggage and school equipment to the riverside. The old school would never see such activity again; we were the last trainees to pass through those halls.

After an early supper we said good-bye to the household staff who had cared for us. They had been some of our first Chinese friends.

It was twilight. We made our way through the city's lanes for the last time. At the wharf we found our things already loaded on the crowded boat. With others, I took my sleeping bag to the flat roof over the pilot's cabin.

Boats anchored beside us danced and bobbed in the

swift water. Half a block away, a single tiny light glowed at the top of the city's old pagoda. A half moon darted in and out of flying clouds.

I had just dozed off when a brightly lit luxury liner drew in for the night. Loud music drowned out the peaceful croaking of frogs. I pulled the hood of my sleeping bag over my head.

An early morning blast from our boat's steam whistle signaled our departure. Cinders showered down. We lurched from the mooring.

At first we churned through lowlands. We passed thatched cottages standing alone in fields of grain. Other houses clustered at the river's edge. Midmorning we steamed into hill country. Low foothills stretched away into purple mountains that rose higher and higher in the distance. We met or passed hundreds of boats.

Sunset brought us to another city. We spent the night in a missionary guest house.

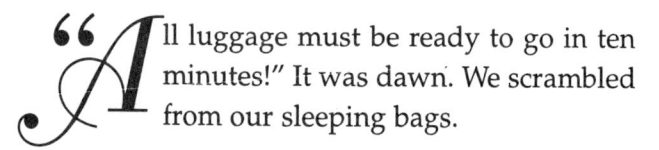

"All luggage must be ready to go in ten minutes!" It was dawn. We scrambled from our sleeping bags.

After breakfast we learned why we had left the language school in Anking. We were going to Kuling Mountain. The mission had recently bought property there.

We climbed into the back of an open truck for a bumpy twelve-mile trip. The truck took us to the foot of the mountain. From there we had to begin our long ascent on foot. We scrambled over rugged terrain. Then we climbed up hundreds of steep steps carved into the mountainside.

Luxuriant jungle covered all but rocky outcroppings. Pink and white wild roses and brilliant azaleas grew everywhere. We saw many waterfalls.

The air cooled quickly as we climbed. Sometimes we rounded sharp curves to see checkerboard fields on the plains far below. People looked like tiny ants in the shimmering distance. *Do they know about Jesus?* I wondered.

Fairy Glen Hotel, our new home, exceeded our wildest imaginations. Only seven days before, the previous owners had sold the hotel to our mission for one U.S. dollar! That included the furniture. They had not seen a future for their hotel in the changing political situation.

For a week we helped with hotel inventory. Then we settled down to study. The break did me good. I pressed on to the written and oral exams.

Evening walks often took us down a short, wooded path. At the end of it stood the temporary primary school for our mission's children.

One day the language students were invited to join the children in their annual sports day. Organizers asked me to be on the softball team. I was delighted. *I may not be good at this language,* I thought, *but I'll show them I can play softball!*

Too many players had been asked for our team but I did not give up my place. At the start of the game I struck a ball and scrambled safely to first base. A teammate followed with a home run. The ground was perfectly smooth. But running ahead of him, I collapsed. My right foot had fractured.

A thought exploded in my head: *You were going to show you could play ball, were you?* I sat out the game. Later teammates carried me back to the hotel.

Others may not have known what God was doing in my life. But I knew. He had touched my foot the way He had touched Jacob's thigh many centuries before. *Will I be a cripple like Jacob the rest of my life,* I wondered, *because of pride?*

For months God had been trying to get my attention. He now had my full attention!

Chapter Twelve

The "Thanksgiving Key"

Four of us new missionaries left to travel together to Chungking in West China. We had finished the first section of our language course.

I was still on crutches. I had to ride down the mountain in a hammock-like chair, suspended between poles. The poles rested on the shoulders of eight carriers. I cringed as we descended, especially on one flight of a thousand steps.

In Chungking I shared a room on the top floor of the mission home. It had a commanding view of the city. From there I watched rich and poor going about their daily tasks. Beyond the crowded tin and tile roofs, I could see the Yangtze River, alive with traffic. It flowed eastward to the Pacific Ocean nearly three thousand miles away.

A student from the nearby Bible seminary had agreed to help me with language study. I needed to change from standard Chinese to the West Sichuan dialect.

One morning I found her waiting. I meant to apologize: "Sorry to keep you waiting, I've just washed my hair."

For a moment she stared at my tousled head. Then she fell back on my bed, rolling with laughter. Instead of the word for human hair, I had used the word for horse hair or feathers! I laughed with her, though I wondered if I would ever learn to speak Chinese correctly.

Summer. The heat and humidity in the river valley grew oppressive. We moved to a vacation bungalow in the hills beyond the river.

It had been a year of constant change. Each change caused a different kind of stress. I needed rest. In the new vacation atmosphere, I found I could not force myself to spend hours studying every day.

My foot still hurt as I hobbled about. I felt hemmed

in. I wanted to roam the hills and communicate in the new language.

Troubling thoughts crowded my mind: *I'll never make it! Why am I here? It would be better to go home now rather than waste more of my time and the mission's money.* The next moment I wanted with all my heart to stay.

It helped to share my anxiety with senior workers there on vacation. They understood—they had traveled this road before me.

In the end, the messages at a summer Bible conference shone the spotlight on the real problem. The speaker emphasized the need to die to self.

I did not want to believe it. I resisted. Then, after days of struggle, my defenses crumbled. I confessed my sinful attitudes to God. I felt humbled, but warmed by God's love. I rekindled my promise and went on.

"Do not be anxious about anything," Paul wrote to the Christians at Philippi, "but in everything by prayer and petition, *with thanksgiving,* present your requests to God. And the peace of God, which transcends all understanding, will guard your hearts and minds in Christ Jesus" (Phil. 4:6, 7).

Giving thanks in the middle of difficult situations? Is that really God's way to free me from anxiety? For me to have peace? I wondered.

I chose to accept God's words. When I did, thanksgiving unlocked doors that had been closed by anxiety. I called it my "thanksgiving key." Learning how and when to use it would take a lot of work.

Chapter Thirteen

When the Key Doesn't Turn

*N*ear the end of the summer, I was invited to lead morning devotions with the household workers. I practiced my message on any senior missionary I could badger into listening. It took three minutes! The Chinese workers had listened to many first-time efforts. They declared they understood.

They were generous. They had probably heard the Zacchaeus story so many times, they knew what *should* be said!

By the end of August the days turned hot—even in the hills. In the terraced fields the rice changed to copper brown.

Many evenings everyone sat outside under starlit skies, hoping to catch a breeze. We watched the lights of Chungking city begin to twinkle in the darkness below. Usually someone would start to sing—or pray—before we went in.

It was time to close the vacation bungalow for the season. I felt sad. God had done a deep work in my life during those weeks, and I was truly grateful.

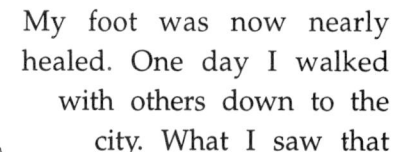

My foot was now nearly healed. One day I walked with others down to the city. What I saw that morning showed me how little I knew the real China. Along the narrow footpaths, tiny piles of ash grew under sticks of smoking incense. People had put them there to beg the gods to hold back the rains until rice could be harvested.

By midday we reached the river. While we waited for a ferry, I saw something I will never forget. From the corner of my eye I noticed people stepping around something. Looking closer, I saw a man. He lay at the water's edge. His eyes were wild with fear and he struggled to breathe. The crowds hurried by. No one offered to help. No one seemed disturbed. I caught the words, "beggar" or "criminal" from some who saw the look on my face.

Maybe, I thought, *but he is a person with a soul.*

The ferry came. The crowd surged forward. Someone called my name. I, too, passed by.

I gripped the handrail. The distance widened between us and the dying man, now alone on the sand. How soon the water would wash his body away, I wondered? In my heart I cried, *When, Lord? When will I be able to help people like that?*

A few weeks later five of us boarded a small upriver steamer. It was a cool autumn evening. We were bound for my first inland home.

We had tickets for cabins, but we found all cabins full. The cheerful captain assured us there would be accommodations. "Just wait until those who have come to see friends off leave the boat," he said.

We huddled together on the windy prow, waiting for an exodus that never came.

By midnight we felt chilled and tired. We followed others down a rope ladder. On the pontoon to which we were anchored, we found a more sheltered spot.

We four women snuggled together in two sleeping bags and tried to rest. Our male escort sat with his back against the side of a grunting hog to keep warm. The hog was tied in a long wicker basket and would be loaded the next morning.

Before dawn we climbed back onto the boat to look for the promised cabin. The cabins had been overbooked. To make room for us in front of his cabin, the pilot pushed some sleeping bodies closer together. The space did not allow us to lie down, but we appreciated the wall as a backrest.

I was getting a nasty cold and I let misery engulf me. Romantic ideas of missionary life began to fade. A long day followed.

That night we anchored beside a small freighter. Our escort persuaded the owner to let us sleep on his small craft. The floor was rough and uneven, but we enjoyed the luxury of just *stretching out*!

A second weary day followed. That evening we hoped for another place to lie flat. When the anchor went down midstream, our hopes sank with it.

Then we saw others making for the roof and ventured after them. We found a vacant space near the center of the slanting roof. There we rigged up a flannel sheet above us. Tying one end of our canopy to the smoke stack, we guiltily tied the other to a sign that read, "Unauthorized persons not allowed on the roof."

When day broke the crew stoked up the boilers. Within seconds fine black soot floated down on us. We grabbed our graying bedding and fled below.

I have seldom heard sweeter words than "Next stop, Luhsien!" I had tried, without great success, to use my "thanksgiving key." Now we had arrived at our new home. Some medicine, a bath and a light supper made it easier.

When I finally climbed into a warm bed piled with soft blankets, the key turned easily. Before drifting off to sleep, I wondered if I would ever learn to use that key in the middle of difficult situations. The years ahead would give plenty of chances to find out.

Chapter Fourteen
Teacher Ho

*M*y new mission family included senior workers Ron and Gwen Roberts and two single workers, jolly Mildred Schroder and reserved Dorothy North. They were all Australian. Studious Pearl McCullough and I were the newcomers. We added Irish and American to the household.

Others on the compound soon became family too. The oldest staff member was Teacher Ho. She was a gracious and tireless woman who worked with women and children. We lovingly called her Ho-Ho.

Philip was a young Chinese pastor from eastern China. Andrew was his local assistant. They directed ministry to the adults in the church.

An elderly widow who sold vegetables for a living, had a room next to Teacher Ho's kitchen. She was not a staff member, but she supported the ministry. Like the Anna in Luke 2, she served God faithfully by fasting and prayer. So we called her Anna.

Brother One was our cook. Brother Two was his brother, and our water carrier and gardener. The short, sturdy gatekeeper and his family completed the number living on the mission compound.

*T*he church in Luhsien was started fifty years earlier. It had grown into the center of a county-wide outreach. Teacher Ho had labored beside many of the early pioneers. Nationals and missionaries alike honored and respected her. All who knew her welcomed her into their homes.

With a basket of eggs or fruit on her arm, she went to encourage and pray with the sick, blind, and needy. She often took me with her. From her I learned Chinese Christian ethics and etiquette.

Teacher Ho kept her silver-flecked black hair pulled into a tight bun at the nape of her neck. Sparkling eyes peered from her round, pleasant face. A birth injury had left her with a slight limp and a weakness on the left side. She never complained, though. Nor did she let the handicap prevent her from ministering to others.

From my room I often saw Ho-Ho in the shaded alley behind her home. She would be bent over a wooden washtub doing her laundry. Across the tub, a young girl or woman would squat on a low stool, learning from the gentle teacher. Sometimes a cooing baby, wrapped in red, lay securely tied in a chair nearby. Often the student leaned toward Teacher Ho, pointing to a forgotten character in the New Testament. I shall never know how many illiterate women and girls learned to read over that washtub. Many who lived near Luhsien's west gate owed their prized reading ability to that teacher in a faded blue gown.

I learned many valuable lessons sitting in on Teacher Ho's Sunday school class. Boys and girls listened attentively as she told Bible stories. She never raised her voice to discipline. I usually didn't notice the problem before she quietly told the disruptive child to leave. The next week he usually returned to sit in the front row. During the week she had visited the child's home. She never invited me along on *those* visits. She did not want the child's parents to "lose face" before a foreigner.

Ho-Ho helped me a lot with language learning. She patiently corrected my wrong words and tones until I could say them right. Once I nearly cried from the effort. "Am I being too hard?" she asked. "Would you like me not to correct you?"

If others had kept after me as much, my problems would not have continued so long.

*M*y earliest opportunity for regular minstry was a children's meeting. It took place at a soap factory a couple of miles upriver. An elder from the church was a foreman at the factory.

Teacher Ho helped me prepare a simple story to give before she told the Bible story. That way she could explain what I meant if I made a mistake.

If the weather was fine, we liked to walk to the factory. Little scouts usually watched for us. As we came into view, they ran toward us. "Jesus is coming!" they shouted to their friends. "Jesus is coming!"

"May it be so!" came Teacher Ho's soft response. Then she welcomed the children who raced up to her. Grasping her good hand, they led us on, eager for the story time.

I learned conversational Chinese as I got to know the older Sunday school girls. They often came to chat. "We see you just sit and look at books all day," they said, "so we've come to visit. Aren't you bored?"

Sometimes the visits were long and kept me from studying. If I tried to explain that I needed to "look" at books to learn their language, they usually responded, "Oh, we'll help you!" They didn't understand that their chatter didn't help prepare me for language exams.

If their visits came too often, dear Ho-Ho would come to the rescue. Calling to my visitors, she would ask them to run an errand or help her with an urgent job—one she had probably just thought up!

I quickly joined the ranks of those who loved and valued Teacher Ho's guidance and wisdom.

Chapter Fifteen

The Threat of War

We moved into 1949. The conquering communist army fanned southward and westward. We heard rumors everywhere. Some were false, some true.

Early that year our Australian seniors left for their furlough. Fred and May Purchas, an English couple with many years of experience in China, replaced them.

CIM leaders thought we should stay as long as we could still encourage the church and point people to Jesus Christ. The Lord would give me two more years of service in Luhsien—and two more years of refining.

In the months before occupation, the national currency was devalued over and over. This affected us more than any other hardship. Money that could buy ten kilos of rice one day might get only half as much a day later.

Rice became a more stable medium of exchange. Like our neighbors, we converted our money into rice. Later, we traded it for other things when we needed them.

Foreigners leaving West China often passed through

our city. They came to us for a place to stay. Some families had to wait many days, which taxed our resources. Yet over and over we saw God provide just at the right time.

One night five visitors stopped. They expected to travel on the next day. They were taking a van to a mission hospital several hundred miles north. The afternoon they arrived, a telegram came. It told them to cancel their trip and return to Chungking. The money they carried met our urgent needs. Telegrams often arrived late those days, but that one came right on time!

God provided for us in many ways. Once we had been waiting for money wired from Shanghai for three weeks. Then we found a pair of gum-rubber boots in our attic. When we sold the boots, they "fed us" until a local bank had the cash to pay us the wired money.

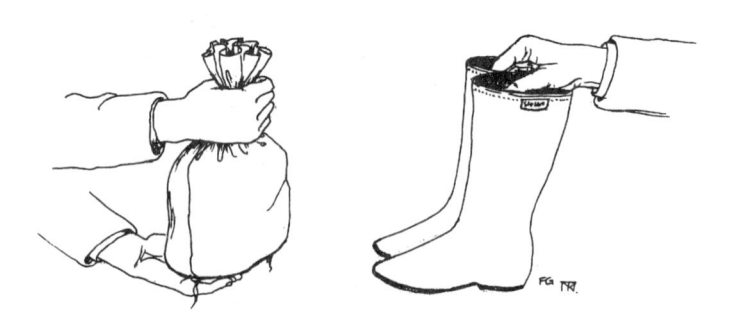

Normal life began to crumble. Bewildered people came for comfort and advice. Night by night they crowded into the tiny street chapel. Sunday school teachers taught scores of children and adults.

On Easter, the Sunday school children repeated in unison the verses they had learned during the year.

Proud adults beamed as they listened to the Word of God from the lips of their children and grandchildren.

I sensed a greater intensity at the short-term Bible school that spring. The students sometimes wondered, aloud, "Is this our last chance to study together?"

I found those months satisfying and busy. But recurring bouts of malaria wore down my health. The district nurse told me to go to a cooler climate as soon as possible.

I could not travel alone. It looked like I would have to wait until summer vacation. Then others would head to the mountains.

Late one evening a fellow missionary arrived by boat from Chungking. Irene Cunningham, with her young son Gordon, had gone to the big city so Gordon could have his tonsils out. They were on their way to their home in the mountains. Irene invited me to travel with them and spend the summer there.

One morning while waiting for transportation, we joined a noisy crowd at the riverside. They had gathered to watch the annual boat races. We mingled with the jostling crowd, chatting and giving away gospel tracts and Scripture portions. Before the final race, our cook came looking for us. Two trucks were leaving for the mountains early the next morning.

Chapter Sixteen

A Visit to Tribal Land

We went home immediately, packed, ate an early supper, and hurried to the river. We arrived in time to make the two-hour crossing to a village near the truck stop.

Before we disappeared into an unkept inn for the night, one of the drivers approached us. "We plan to leave before dawn," he whispered. "We want to escape 'yellow fish.' "

He meant unpaying passengers. They were often deserters from the army. These men would refuse to budge from their perches once they had climbed onto the back of a loaded vehicle.

That night an unexpected attack of malaria sent my temperature soaring. There was no way to get to the medicine. It was packed in bags buried in the depths of those overloaded trucks. It was a long night.

We left well before sunrise, but we did not completely escape the "yellow fish."

If I had not been so ill, I might have enjoyed the eleven-hour trip. We bounced over a narrow road that followed a turbulent, winding river.

Nightfall brought us to the home of Walter and Helen Jespersen. Walter was Irene's brother. We had planned to spend one night there, but I was too ill to travel on. Irene and Gordon went on as planned. I remained behind.

*T*wenty-four days later the Jespersens judged me well enough to go the last twenty-eight miles to the mountain home of the Cunninghams. Edith Jackson, whom I had met in language school, lived with the Jespersens. She would accompany me.

The day we planned to go, we learned we had a problem. All the men who usually carried passengers to the hills had been booked for the funeral of a big official. They would not be available for several days.

Someone suggested we hire freight carriers. These men usually carry coal, fuel oil, or slab salt into the mountains. "My men are reliable, honest, and do not smoke opium," boasted the manager of the carriers we hired. "They can easily get you there in a day."

We began to question his promises when we saw the men who came to carry us. Then we saw the makeshift chairs they brought us to ride in!

We left the mission compound in pelting rain. Great drops of rain spattered right through the coarse canopies over our heads. The men stopped every hour for rest and food. Around noon we turned off the narrow stone road. Then we headed up into more rugged terrain.

When one of my carriers stumbled, I climbed down to give the men a break. At last I could see the magnificent surroundings. But the men did not want to "lose face." They urged me back into the chair. With reluctance, I returned to my view of the sky.

By afternoon some of the men dallied longer at each stop. The sweet smell of opium told us the problem. Fellow carriers urged the stragglers on. They responded with sullen looks. We knew they could "accidentally" drop us over a cliff if they chose. We prayed earnestly for protection and safety!

We came to many forks in the path. The carriers argued about which way to take. Twice they wanted to stop at lonely farmhouses. We urged them on.

By late afternoon a storm gathered over distant peaks. We rounded a sharp curve and gazed across a deep, partly-cultivated valley. A cluster of buildings lay on the far side. Our hearts leapt. The carriers hurried on.

Nearing the settlement, we realized we had not found what we were looking for. It was a small tribal community. As we stopped in front of the largest building, the storm broke. Darkness closed in.

Chapter Seventeen

Tribal Hospitality

Villagers rushed us through a walled courtyard to shelter. Only one light shone in the thick darkness. It glowed from graying embers in a fire-pit at the center of the large room. Someone dropped a handful of dried sticks on the smoldering ashes. The flames leapt upward.

The light revealed a crush of onlookers. An older woman motioned for us to shed our wet coats. Giggling girls touched our hands, felt our wool sweaters, and pressed strands of our hair between their fingers.

When our sleeping bags appeared, people exclaimed in wonder. The more curious lit sticks of bamboo at the fire to examine the bags more closely. Amazement grew when we unzipped them and spread them on a bed to dry.

A blackened kettle on the fire came quickly to a boil. Before long we sipped hot black tea.

The kind matriarch pushed aside strings of peppers, onions, and tobacco drying over the bed to make room for our mosquito nets. That gave us our cue to go to bed.

I pulled out a Scripture booklet to read by the dim light. The curious folk gathered to see it. One of the girls brought a burning stick and sat down beside me. "This book," I said, "has words from the God in heaven. It's in my language, but we have one in Chinese. Would you like to see it?"

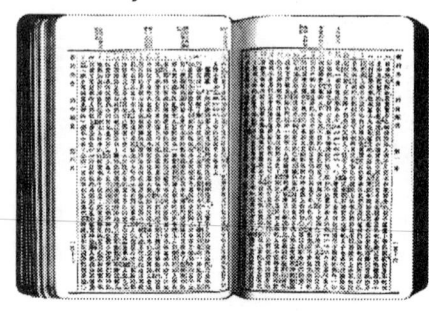

She nodded eagerly. The family crowded closer as I pulled out a Chinese Gospel of John. Turning to John 3:16, I read—or rather recited—the very first Bible verse we had learned in Chinese. At first the group said they could not understand me. When I repeated the verse again and again, they began to say it after me.

They understand! I thought, rejoicing.

"Can anyone here read Chinese?" Edith asked.

A shy lad acknowledged that he could. His grandmother beamed. We gave him the book, and he promised to read it to the others.

"Do you pray to your God?" someone asked.

"Yes, we do," we replied.

"Show us how," our listeners urged.

Edith responded with the Lord's Prayer. We'd also learned it for our first language exam. She continued and gave thanks for those who had welcomed us into their home. How we longed for more language to respond to their questions!

For a time, people chatted quietly around the fire. They examined whatever we had left outside our nets.

They tried on our shoes and coats. They sampled water from our canteens. Then, one by one, as they finished their smokes, they left the room. We zipped ourselves into our damp sleeping bags.

I thanked my heavenly Father for His care through the day and for shelter now in this home. Rain pattered on the roof. Baby ducklings peeped in a basket across the room. Cattle and hogs snored just beyond a half door. A couple of times in the night, Granny came into the room to look around and check the fire.

The household stirred at dawn. The carriers did not appear until much later. Edith and I gratefully accepted the flat corn cakes and black tea brought to us.

Our carriers were not used to such food. They refused it. Without rice and opium, they grumbled and dallied.

By nine o'clock the sun had spread across the valley floor, so we said good-bye to our open-hearted hosts. We had not gone far, however, before the men insisted they could no longer carry us. Walking the rest of the trail, we reached "Gospel Mountain" just before noon.

Missionary children and their little tribal friends ran to meet us as we picked our way down the last steep incline. "Why didn't you come last night?" they wanted to know.

"Ah, that's a long story! We'll tell you all about it later." Those stories made good nap-time tales for many days!

Rest, healthy food, walks in the mountain air, and old-fashioned quinine, along with a new drug called

Atabrine, finally conquered my chilling fevers.

*F*rom the window of my room above the Gospel Hall I watched nimble, barefoot men and women. They wore patched, tattered clothing as they worked the craggy slopes. I enjoyed their lively chatter and the laughter of their children. It made me long to get to know these people.

I found my tribal neighbors light-hearted and happy. Over one hundred gathered for their annual Bible conference. Some came from fifty miles away! I watched them arriving, some descending from high mountain passes. Each brought a week's supply of food, mostly ground corn, in a basket on his or her back.

Their singing delighted me. Bursts of harmony, when the sopranos and tenors lilted up to the highest notes, sent chills up and down my spine. I loved being awakened by their melodies.

As these folk listened to the messages, I could sense their hunger for God's Word. The last day of conference began as usual with an hour of prayer. Then, while shadows still lingered in the valley, we walked a mile to a sparkling pool at the base of a waterfall. We went there for the baptism of an elderly couple and eight others.

The last afternoon a pastor from a neighboring tribal group gave the challenge to a hushed audience. I sat among them. At the end of the service we shared bread and wine, symbols of our Savior's death for us. It confirmed the unity we have in Jesus Christ, in spite of race, culture or background. I wondered if one day I would share such unity with Nosu people. I hoped so.

    I would have liked to stay right there and minister among those charming mountain people. But quickly changing political events meant I must return to Luhsien.

Chapter Eighteen

Ministry in the Valley

I found the autumn Bible school in progress in Luhsien. Once a week I joined some of the students and staff on a walk to a tiny chapel five miles from the city. The three-sided structure stood in a grove of trees on the crest of a hill. A local Christian family had given the land for it.

Each morning hundreds of farmer folk with baskets of fresh produce passed the little shelter. They were on the way to city markets. We arrived about noon, when the people began to return home. Many stopped to rest in the shade. Dippers hung from a bamboo trough. It brought cool water from a nearby spring. The farmers sat chatting on backless benches or on carrying poles laid across their empty baskets. Some gathered around to read the posters and gospel tracts we fastened to the mud walls.

Some produce-sellers strolled over to the chapel. There they listened to the students give short messages and sing. Others listened from a distance. After taking a short rest, people were usually ready to move on. New arrivals took their places.

We recognized some who stopped week by week. Others hurried by with heads turned away. Most gladly received the gospel literature we offered. A few bought our colorful Scripture posters to put on the plain walls of their homes. Latecomers, usually those with unsold goods, stopped only for a cold drink.

Around three in the afternoon, we gathered up the remaining literature. The men hoisted the benches onto their shoulders. Then we made our way along a narrow path between paddy fields to the farmhouse. The family at the farmhouse had a hot, tasty meal ready. Not even piglets sleeping near the doorway could ruin our appetites for that late lunch! Nor did we mind the dogs and chicks waiting at our feet for dropped bits of food. Ducks, chickens, geese, and water buffalo roamed freely about stacks of straw in the freshly swept farmyard. On high racks near the house, flat bamboo trays of peanuts and soybeans dried in the afternoon sun. Little did we know that this peaceful scene would turn to devastation before a year had passed.

After the meal we committed to God the scattered Seed we had sown. Then we turned homeward.

A large military complex had moved from the east coast ahead of the rapidly moving communist army. They relocated a few miles downriver from us. A number of Christian employees moved with the installation.

We learned about the group when they came to ask for someone to come teach them. Philip, the young pastor, and our senior missionary, Fred, responded gladly.

One day illness kept Fred home. I went in his place. Pastor Tzang, an older teacher at the short-term Bible school, would preach in the morning. I was to teach Fred's afternoon English Bible class.

The friends from the government complex came to show us the way. We traveled in rickshaws over mucky streets alive with morning shoppers. At the far end of the city our escorts found a boat to take us downriver. After haggling over the price, we climbed aboard.

The swift current took only twenty minutes to carry us to the small village. Our friends had canvas carrying chairs waiting. At the gates of the huge military factory we gained entrance without question, in spite of tight security.

Over fifty adults listened attentively to the pastor's message. Someone had written out the songs on a blackboard. The people sang warmly, though off-key.

After the meeting we chatted until lunch. At one-thirty, with pounding heart, I stepped into a well-filled room. I gave a short, well-practiced introduction in Chinese. Then I began my Bible study in English. These highly qualified men and women understood me well. I felt an immediate rapport with them.

As soon as the class finished, we needed to head

home. It was November, and the days were growing short. A trip against the current still lay ahead of us.

Pastor Tzang climbed into his chair, and I stepped into mine. But when the men lifted me, the canvas split! Three quarters of the seat tore from the back rest!

The pastor had already gone well beyond the gate. The factory workers called to stop him. He returned as the carriers quickly laced ropes around the frame. "Try again!" they invited. This time the canvas ripped away completely!

We could do nothing. We had to wait for another chair. When we finally reached the river, I realized how serious our delay was. "No boats going upriver tonight," someone told us.

Our carriers would go no farther. "The path along the river is too bad to travel in the dark," they said.

Evil-minded bystanders flung insults at my chaperone. "Where are you going with a foreign woman this time of the evening?" they called. Pastor Tzang ignored their crude taunts.

Then someone spotted a boat a little distance upriver. It was just pushing off. Calling to the boatmen, we hurried down slick steps and ran along the water's edge to the craft. There were no other women on the boat. The pastor asked three men seated next to the side of the boat to scoot toward the center. Then I could sit on the outside. He did not sit down until I had laid my Bible on the seat between us. Pastor Tzang knew our more relaxed Western ways, but would not compromise his own culture.

We made slow progress upriver. Twice, at swirling rapids, we all got out. Other passengers scrambled to the tow ropes. When I moved to help, the pastor motioned me away. "You are a foreign teacher, a guest in our country," he said. "It's not fitting for you to do such tasks." Then he added, "Just as a woman is not to sit touching a man, neither is she to have her hand on the same rope with a man's hand."

I followed demurely behind. So that's why he had extended the handle of his umbrella to help me down those slippery steps! I wondered how many other *faux pas* I had made that day. I began to understand why the older man had come to escort me instead of the young pastor. I felt thankful to be learning Chinese customs from a true Christian gentleman.

Chapter Nineteen

As the Storm Gathers

Later I learned of something else that happened that day. Rachel was one of those who had shown us the way from the river. I had chatted with her as we waited for lunch at the factory. Several children played around us. "Is anyone teaching these children about Jesus?" I asked.

"No," she replied. "Won't you come teach them?"

"I'd like that," I said, "but my language is not good enough. Maybe one day I can. Why don't you teach them?"

"I'm not qualified," she said. "Besides, I have no teaching materials."

At that moment, we were called to lunch. We could talk no more. But I felt burdened to pray. Five days later Rachel came to visit. Her first words thrilled me. "God has told me to teach the children. Will you help me prepare?"

With Teacher Ho's help, the next Sunday the children at the government factory heard about Jesus.

I looked forward to returning to the factory to encourage Rachel with her class. It would never happen. Within a few weeks the Communists came. That factory was one of the first to fall into their hands.

*I*n spite of uncertainty, the autumn Bible school continued to the end of term. As usual, it closed with the annual county-wide conference for all believers.

Some of those who came stayed with relatives in the city. Most wanted the extra hours of Christian fellowship with old friends. They stayed on the church compound.

The first afternoon of the conference a telegram arrived. It advised the main speaker to return to Chungking. After prayer, however, he chose to stay. His quiet example of faith in God encouraged others.

The last evening, a communion service brought the conference to a triumphant end. Afterwards people gathered in little groups in the church or in other rooms. They asked God to make them strong, wise, and faithful. Many talked and prayed into the early morning hours.

We rose well before daybreak to say good-bye to speakers, teachers, students and guests. As we bowed to pray with those who were leaving, a hush always settled over the people standing nearby. Several times I heard the words, "Look! The Christians are praying that God will keep them safe." We did pray for safety. But we prayed more for God to guard the hearts of our friends and keep them true to Himself through the days ahead.

Chapter Twenty

Liberation

Quiet fell over the empty mission compound. Two mornings later even the streets outside grew silent. City residents fled to the country. Country people slipped into the city. The compound gateman kept the big front gates closed.

The stillness deepened. I was embroidering the cover of a bag for Teacher Ho's Christmas. It gave my hands something to do and left my mind free to talk with the Lord.

"How would you like to learn how to make real English Christmas cake and pudding today?" May asked at breakfast the next morning.

"Super!" I answered. It would help quiet the tension in our hearts.

We spent the morning preparing the fruit. After lunch we blended the mixtures and put them to bake and steam.

Mid-afternoon I went to the kitchen to test the cake. Just then, a far-off sputter of artillery broke the stillness. Peering out the windows, we saw soldiers running among the orange trees beyond the river. The conquest of Luhsien had begun.

We had decided to read a book at meal times to keep from talking about the war. Fred had just picked up the book. Suddenly, exploding shells rattled windows and shook the house. We looked at our reader, wondering what to do. Fred's nod sent us flying down the steps to street level. Ho-Ho, Anna, Philip, and Andrew had already gathered outside. We prayed together. Then we waited, talking softly.

Twice the bombing stopped. Then it erupted again. Finally a silence settled over the city. We finally felt safe enough to return to our house and went inside.

Our half-finished supper still cluttered the dining table. In the kitchen the well-steamed pudding sat in a dry pot on a cold stove. *Is this how things will look to those left behind when the Lord returns?* I wondered.

All remained quiet. Even so, we decided to bring bedding from the upstairs rooms. We made up beds on the office floor for the night and lay down fully dressed.

About two hours passed. Then what sounded like an old-fashioned Fourth of July jolted us awake. "Your emancipators have come!" we heard town criers shout. "Open your gates! Come! Welcome them!"

Scrambling from my makeshift bed, I followed others to the front of the compound. Gatey stood trembling in the darkness. His hand was on the great latch of the big wooden doors. "Don't open them yet!" called Fred. "Stand by; we'll go upstairs to see what is going on."

We climbed the narrow steps in the gatehouse. Its rooms had recently held conference guests. We cautiously unlocked the shutters and peered out.

The criers carried flaming torches. They dashed in and out of dark lanes and alleys with their message. A babbling mob spewed into the street below. I looked at my watch. It was just past midnight, December 4, 1949.

Suddenly, the babble of voices organized into a synchronized chant of welcome to the conquerors. Then we saw them! Down the street seven young soldiers marched in single file, twelve paces apart. Their carbines swung easily at their sides. Except for the leader, each soldier wore a nationalist army uniform with jacket and cap turned inside out. Each crumpled cap sported a newly attached red star.

I shivered. The hubbub faded as the parade moved on, toward the city center. We closed the windows and went downstairs. "We will leave the gates closed," Fred told Gatey, "at least until daylight."

We mounted the broad steps past the church. "Come in and sit a while," called Teacher Ho over her shoulder.

Ho-Ho poured each of us a cup of hot water from a thermos. We nibbled watermelon seeds and warmed our hands on the cups. A tiny flame hissed from the wick in a shallow bowl of oil on the table. It cast flickering shadows across tired faces. We bowed to give thanks for safety—then the room grew silent. Each of us wondered how our new "liberties" would develop.

Only God knew the future. He would remain true to His promise: "I will never leave you or forsake you."

I asked Him to keep me true to mine.

Chapter Twenty-One
"Liberties"

Life on the streets returned to normal—on the surface. Only a few adults came to the worship service that Sunday morning. Not one child turned up for Sunday school. The next day schools plunged into preparations for a new government holiday.

Heavy rains delayed the celebrations until two days before Christmas. We watched school children in new uniforms goose-step proudly behind marching bands. They shouted the slogans printed on huge red banners they carried. Pictures of Marx, Lenin, and Stalin hung everywhere.

Our Christmas service was quieter than usual. But it still brought back the joy of Jesus' birthday. A few people came from country churches and the soap factory. No one came from the down-river plant.

The day after Christmas was sunny and clear. It seemed ideal for an outing. We packed a picnic lunch and walked to a famous cliff. Centuries before, someone had carved the story of a famous battle in flowing Chinese characters on the cliff face. Nearby rushed a river. The beauty, fresh air, and fellowship gave us the break we needed.

On our return to the city we nodded to surprised soldiers we met along the way.

Two days later we received visitors from the Foreign Affairs Bureau. "We've come to see how things are for you now," they said. "Is there anything we can do to help you? We want you to feel secure and free from anxiety."

Ending their visit, they added uneasily, "Oh, by the way, we think it best for you not to ramble out into the hills. There could still be enemy soldiers out there, you know."

We got the message.

Early in the new year we became aware of a throbbing rhythm. It continued day and night and had a strange numbing effect.

About the same time communist cadres assigned all able-bodied adults to three different groups. Ten family members made up the first group, and fifty near neighbors the second. One hundred people from a local district formed the third group. These groups would make it easier to indoctrinate the people with the new communist teaching. People had to attend and be active in each group. Group leaders considered excuses only after they received a written request.

Christians often found that their group meetings were at the same time as regular church functions. Church meeting hours were changed. Then the time for group sessions changed again to conflict with the church meeting. It did not seem like a coincidence.

People grew uneasy.

We continued to visit friends in their homes to encourage them. We also kept going to the soap factory for the weekly children's Bible story hour. Then our friends there suggested we stop coming until the soldiers left. The soldiers did not leave.

Worship services, prayer meetings, Bible classes, and baptism class continued into the first quarter of the year. All met at uncertain hours.

The vacation Bible school at Chinese New Year, the last day of February, drew many children.

After about five months, visits from the Bureau of Foreign Affairs increased. Their messages grew firmer. Each visit brought more restrictions. With threats thinly veiled, officials told us, "Our only concern is for your safety."

One day they advised us not to leave the city. "There is trouble in the countryside," they said. We were not surprised. We had heard about landlords being executed as part of land reform. Maybe they didn't want us to see the executions.

We longed to go encourage friends in the country churches. I especially missed our visits to the little wayside chapel on market days.

The day after a regular open-air meeting in town, officials came again. "We still fear for your safety," they said awkwardly. "Hoodlums roam the streets these days. It's all right for you to hold meetings here on your property. But it is best not to hold them elsewhere."

Weeknight meetings in a small gate-house room continued. They attracted people too shy to go up to the main church. A deputation from the police came again. This time the senior officer wore full uniform. "We see ruffians, known by us, coming into your little chapel. You are no longer to hold meetings there. You may hold them in your church, but not in the room that opens onto the street."

The last door for widespread evangelism had closed—just six months after occupation.

Chapter Twenty-Two

Harassed!

Restrictions increased. Opportunities to help needy neighbors withered. One old blind woman often begged her daughter-in-law to have us come visit. Teacher Ho and I promised to go.

Before we entered the home the daughter-in-law glanced anxiously toward a nearby house. It was the home of the local cadre who watched neighborhood activities.

Safely inside, we climbed the familiar steps. Granny lived alone in a far corner of the loft above the kitchen. To keep her from moving about, someone had removed all the floorboards except in her tiny area.

Teacher Ho had brought along some fresh eggs for the woman. She took an egg from her basket and laid it in the gnarled hand. Lifting the treasure to her nose, the old woman smiled a sweet, toothless thanks.

Teacher Ho read Scripture and prayed with her.

Then we picked our way carefully back across the open beams to the steps. We were never able to return.

Officials came day after day to inquire into every area of our personal lives. Their rapid questions had to be answered in detail and on the spot. Our examiners wanted to know the history of our grandparents, parents, brothers and sisters.

"In what year did your grandparents buy land in America? How many acres did they buy? What did they pay for it? Were they very rich? Name all the places your parents ever lived. To which political party does your family belong? To what party do you belong? Have you a communist party in America? Why don't you belong to it? Where did you go to school? Give the dates and length of time at each school. Is your father a landowner? If so, why did you work to pay for your college? What kind of work have you done? What was your wage at each job? List the occupation of each family member. Have you ever been to Russia? Why not? Why did you come to China?" On and on and on!

We were harassed each time we left the compound. Finally we stopped going out unless absolutely necessary. With less opportunity for ministry, I turned more and more to language learning. In particular, I studied the new "in" vocabulary. Even our non-official visitors were using it.

We let our water carrier/gardener go because of limited work and money. Besides, we had more time to do the work ourselves. He begged to stay with us, but we could not keep him.

Brother One, our long-time cook, remained. In fact, our official visitors advised us to keep him on. "As teachers in our country," they said, "you should have such help in your home."

Later we learned Brother One had been assigned to keep an eye on our activities. He had to report them to the Foreign Affairs Bureau. Our loyal helper now walked a difficult path.

The relentless indoctrination meetings began having their intended effect. Fear settled over hearts like a thick cloud. Fewer and fewer people came to church meetings. They were afraid of those who came to "observe" the gatherings.

So few came that we decided to hold services in one of the smaller Sunday school rooms. Shortly after that, representatives from the Promotion Department came to visit the pastor. "Is it true that you no longer use your large church hall? What a great pity for such a building to sit unused!" they said. "It would be a very suitable place for the exhibition we are planning. May we borrow the building for a week?"

Request granted. We had no choice.

Chapter Twenty-Three

Imprisonment and Provision

Workmen came. They whitewashed away the large Chinese characters at the front of the chapel. "Jesus Christ, the Light of the World" was replaced with, "World Communism, Our Hope." Communist mottoes also appeared on side walls.

When the exhibit opened, huge crowds came. Teachers herded their students through the displays. Group leaders came with their groups. Pastor Philip and Andrew, who lived in rooms beside the church, chatted with many visitors. They also gave gospel literature and Scripture portions to any who wanted them.

On the third day the police took the two young men to the station for questioning. "Why," the authorities wanted to know, "are you giving out anti-Communist literature, without permission, at a public exhibit?"

"This is our habit when visitors come to our home," Pastor Philip and Andrew said.

The two were jailed.

Teacher Ho was called to the police station. She learned that she could speak briefly to the prisoners when she brought their daily food.

In the mission house we prayed constantly for our co-workers. Teacher Ho warned us to stay indoors. After each trip to the jail with food, she came to tell us what had happened and to pray.

"If all the literature you gave out is collected and brought to us, we will release you," authorities told the jailed men four days later.

When they told Teacher Ho, she and Anna immediately set out to visit the homes of friends. They asked for any literature they could find. "It doesn't matter when you got it," they said. The two women collected over a hundred pieces of literature and took it to the police station. That evening Philip and Andrew were released.

The very next morning officers came to see the parolees. "You now have a prison record," they said. "Therefore, we must have the complete text of every message you plan to give. It must be written out and submitted three days before it is given."

Obeying that order proved difficult. Yet the men rejoiced. At least one person would read the text of each message. He would also read the Scripture that told God's way of salvation.

The exhibition in the church lasted four weeks. Shortly after it closed another request came to use the building. This time it was from the Housing Commission. "We need more facilities for government workers," the official said. "An unused building like this could easily be made into apartments."

Even before workers finished the remodeling, surveillance workers moved in. They dismissed Gatey, our faithful gate-keeper. He was told to return with his family to the country. Now no one entered or left the compound unseen or unquestioned.

Cash-transfer problems at the post office also stretched our faith. "Well, folks," Fred announced one day at lunch, "Still no money at the post office." He had gone five days in a row. We expected money from CIM in Shanghai.

"Not only that," he went on, "the cook just told me this is the last of our rice. We have no cash to buy more."

We bowed our heads to pray about this urgent need. Just then, we heard a strange sound. Fred went to the front door. Seeing no one, he came back to the table. We continued to pray. The soft tapping came again. "Some prankster out there," Fred said.

He pushed his chair from the table. This time we followed. Cautiously he parted the curtain, then opened the door a crack. Stepping back, he flung open the door and exclaimed, laughing, "Aha! So *you're* the culprit!"

Tied by a string to the doorknob, a fish flapped its tail against the door. We joined the laughter, then looked out to see who had brought it. We saw only a black-slippered heel disappear around a corner. It looked like Ho-Ho's heel. But our dear friend never admitted that she was God's raven. We gave thanks to our heavenly Provider, both for the gift and the one who delivered it.

The next day after his trip to the post office, Fred

burst into the house. "Our money has come!" he called out. We laughed and cried together, thanking God.

Our heavenly Father was teaching us to trust Him more fully. It was a lesson we would all need in the days ahead.

Chapter Twenty-Four

Crucible of Fear

In 1950 Luhsien had an unusually wet and cold summer. Combined with growing tension, it triggered acute arthritis for May. She tried to carry on, but her painful joints needed more medical help than she could get locally.

Fred tried to get the required travel permit to take her to Chungking. He received a firm "No! The only permits being granted to foreigners are to leave the country."

When Fred returned with the bad news, cold fear gripped my heart. To the Lord I cried: "O, Father, how can Dorothy and I stay here alone?" Fred and May had been in China for many years. They knew the language and culture well. Dorothy and I were new and could barely speak the language. "Besides," I ended lamely, "You know we don't get along well. You won't make us stay here alone, will You?"

I did not get my answer right away.

Mission leaders gave Fred and May permission to return to England. At the same time, they arranged for another senior couple to replace them. The authorities refused to grant travel permits to the replacement couple.

May's pain continued, but I found it hard to pray for the exit permits to come quickly. It also seemed impossible to give thanks in the situation. Instead, I begged God to let Dorothy and I go with them.

Looking back now, I can see how the Lord used the situation to test my promise. My "thanksgiving key" lay almost unused. My peace departed. Fears multiplied.

Anna's consistent example shamed me. She was the elderly vegetable seller who lived near Teacher Ho. Her situation was far worse than mine. Yet she kept a quiet peace. She always found something to be thankful for.

As a young bride, she had come with her husband from southeast China. Soon afterwards, her husband died. Too poor to return home, she stayed on alone.

I understood little of her south China dialect, but I learned one of her often-used phrases: *"Gom-she, Ju!"*—"Thank you, Jesus!"

Before dawn every day except Sunday, Anna went to the riverside. There she bought vegetables from farmers bringing produce to market. She hawked them up and down narrow alleys. She usually returned home by noon with a few wilted vegetables for herself. As living conditions grew harder, those limp leaves often hid a little fruit, a small fish, or a bit of meat.

These she had traded for some of her vegetables. She brought them as gifts to one of us on the compound. With a deep bow and a broad smile, she would say, "For God's servants."

Oh, that I had learned to be as accepting and thankful!

Summer turned to autumn. Almost daily we heard shots from the parade grounds just outside the city's west gate. They did not come from the starting gun at a race. And the shouts we heard were not cheers at a game.

Every time I heard those sounds, I remembered a scene I had happened to see one day. I had been returning from the post office. Two men carried a third man. All three were headed for execution.

I should have thanked God I did not have to be a part of the cheering crowd at those executions. Fear stifled thanksgiving.

In mid-November, the day I dreaded came. Fred and May held their exit permits in their hands.

Chapter Twenty-Five

Despair

Before they could make travel plans, Fred and May had to find a local person to be their "guarantor." He would pay any debts discovered after they left. The guarantor would also be responsible for any words Fred and May said that were unfavorable to the new government.

A loyal church elder trusted his missionary friends and agreed to stand. We thanked God for his courage. People could make up accusations that would cost him dearly.

Visits to government offices seemed endless. Someone had to take over signing postal money orders. They would also receive money from the bank. Their signature had to be notarized. Officials needed the name of the new "head of household" and the mission representative.

Fred and May had to publish a "notice of departure" in the local newspaper, three days in a row. This allowed time before they left for people to report grievances to the police. Until they finished all these things, they could not book river tickets.

Fred and May tried to protect Dorothy and me from problems after they left. Fred arranged with a government construction company to get the main house and back garden at the end of the year. The office building at a lower level remained ours. Dorothy and I would live there. We also kept the old storage building across from the offices. A small, grassy lawn separated the two buildings. This area was at the center of the whole mission complex and not far from Teacher Ho's quarters. We hoped it would give us some privacy and safety.

Before Fred and May finished all their arrangements, a telegram came from Dr. Jim Broomhall. He asked me to come immediately to Nosu territory. He wanted me to help in the medical work there. I had been assigned to join that ministry and I wanted to go. But the move was now impossible.

The next day an even more jolting telegram arrived. It came from our mission headquarters in Shanghai. "We advise all missionary personnel to evacuate," it said.

God has answered my prayers! I thought. I cried for sheer joy. Now we could all go together!

I was wrong.

Fred asked if he and May could delay their departure until Dorothy and I received our exit permits. The answer was brusque. "You have asked to leave the country. If you do not go now, your travel passes might be cancelled indefinitely."

They could not risk the possibility. They would have to leave without us.

Eight days before Christmas they left. Dorothy and others from the compound went to the wharf to see them off. I didn't trust myself not to cry. I said good-bye to them at home. After seeing them off in rickshaws at the front gate, I fled back into the empty house.

Work would keep me rational, I thought. There was plenty of that! In fourteen days we had to have everything out of the sixty-year-old mission house.

I let myself wander back into the dining room. There, as a family, we had often shared, prayed together, and claimed promises from God's Word. *We won't need such a large table now*, I thought. I started to remove a board. Instead, I crumpled onto it. "I can't—I can't go on," I sobbed into the emptiness.

But the room was not empty. God was there.

Chapter Twenty-Six

Surprises in the Attic

*A*n hour or so later, I heard the others return. I fled to the attic with my red, swollen eyes and began to work there.

"We're back," Dorothy called from the foot of the stairs. "I'm going to the office to work on accounts." Dorothy had her own quiet way of working off anguish.

Mine was plowing into the things left behind by generations of former residents.

With a crash I tossed discards from the outside attic door. They fell to the ground two floors below. Brother One heard the racket and came to see what was going on. He stayed to help.

Here we found a pair of crutches, there an old-fashioned dress form. Beside them rested rusty metal frames. They had once been used to stretch and dry heavy wool stockings. At the far side of the attic a wicker baby basket and a couple of battered trunks stood beside a bent bicycle wheel. What stories could those things have told about the people who once lived in this old home?

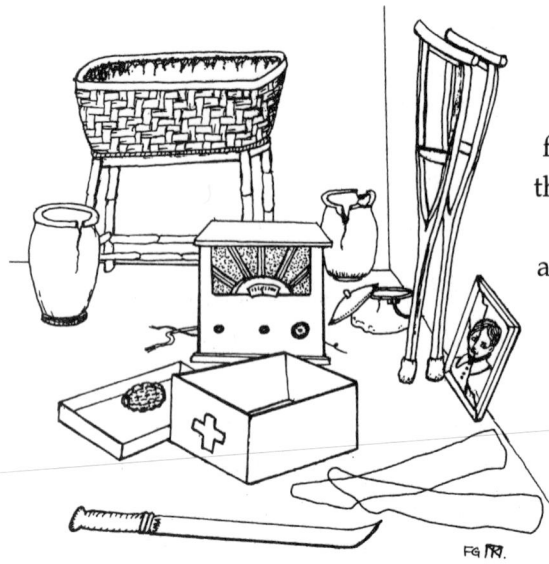

As we continued, I found a machete on the floor. "What is this?" I asked.

"Oh, that! It's a jungle knife," answered the cook. "We used it to cut down banana trees and hack out brambles in the back garden."

I took the long knife to the doorway for a closer look. With horror, I saw an insignia that identified it as a military weapon. "We will have to take this to the police," I told Brother One. I remembered an early law of the new government. All weapons had to be turned in.

"Oh, no—you can't do that!" he objected. "It must be destroyed."

My confidence in our cook rose a notch. I carried the weapon to my bedroom and buried it in a drawer.

Our mission leaders had told us to leave the property clean and in good order. Nothing that could incriminate us must remain. That included personal photos, letters, books, and maps—even maps in old Bibles.

"Whatever can we do with all these things?" I groaned.

"Well," the cook suggested, "the wooden things can

be split into kindling. Those broken window panes and mirrors can be sold. The cracked water jars, leaky kettles, and old lids will probably sell too."

Appreciation for my loyal helper went up another step!

In a far corner among other cast-offs we found a radio with no dial. It had dangling, corroded wires. The cook eyed it with interest. "Umm, I might be able to sell some of that for spare parts."

"You will take care, won't you?" I warned.

Brother One nodded. I was glad we had not known about the old radio before. We had been asked over and over about equipment that could receive or send messages to the United States. We had told them in all sincerity, "No, we have none." Our interrogators never seemed to believe us.

A warning flashed in my brain. *Don't forget, Brother One is expected to report everything to the Foreign Affairs Bureau. He could make a nasty situation out of this.*

We kept at our task. Darkness had nearly closed in when I came upon a shoe-box-sized carton with a Red Cross label. Something heavy rolled inside as I picked it up. Opening it, I wondered aloud what the oval-shaped hunk of scored metal could be.

"Oh, that's a Japanese hand grenade," Brother One replied casually. Seeing the shock on my face, he added, "Don't worry. The pin is out! Soldiers brought it to show the pastor a long time ago, after the war."

Chills tingled up and down my spine. I thought of what tomorrow's headlines might say: "*U.S. missionary hiding deadly weapons and sending secret clandestine messages to Washington"*!

I took the second offender to my bedroom. *What else will we find?* I wondered. That night I went to bed emotionally and physically drained.

Early the next morning the cook went to market as usual. I wrestled in prayer. Would he report the discoveries? He returned alone and came to find me. "We must dispose of that jungle knife and grenade today," he said.

That evening, others gathered for the prayer service. I slipped into a warm coat and brought the machete and hand grenade from my room. The cook went for the hoe. "We will bury the grenade first," he said.

But where?

We decided on a sheltered corner in the back garden. I fiddled with the cold, iron ball in my pocket while the cook dug a hole. Kneeling, I laid the grenade in the pit. Brother One raked the freshly disturbed earth back and covered it with leaves.

Back in the kitchen, we decided the machete must be cut into pieces. Doing it was another matter!

With every thrust of the hacksaw, the hard steel screeched into the still night air. We stopped each time, afraid of listening ears.

Finally the long monster lay in four pieces. Three of them we took to the garden. We drove the pieces deep into the ground beside gnarled tree roots. The remaining piece we put in the stove. Its fiber handle had to be burned off. Later, when our efforts to file away the "U.S. Army" insignia only made it brighter, we buried it under a flagstone in the kitchen floor.

We cleaned up the filings and put away the saw and file. Then we paused to thank God for closing the ears of those who might cause trouble. "Lord, don't let our infractions ever cause trouble to anyone again," we prayed.

One problem remained. The cook had once mentioned seeing a gun. It had been offered to a former missionary. Mission policy forbade keeping firearms. I doubted he had accepted the gift. But we needed to be sure. The next few days we searched everywhere. Finally we decided the gun had either been refused or gotten rid of.

But if Brother One should decide to talk, it would not be so easy to dispose of his words.

Chapter Twenty-Seven

Christmas Comes Late

We continued to clear out the old house. At Ho-Ho's suggestion, we offered bedding, clothes, and household equipment for sale at give-away prices.

After three days the police came to investigate. "Do you have a merchant's license?" they asked. "If not, what you are doing is illegal. It must be stopped immediately."

"What should we do now?" we wondered. We could not give stuff away. That would be seen as bribery. People would be punished for accepting the gifts. But we could not leave personal things behind.

Two large clay stoves solved our problem. They were normally used to boil laundry on wash days. Day after day, we stoked the flames with things our friends could have used. We also threw in books we would have liked to take with us.

We fanned the fires so there would be less smoke. As we did, we prayed no one would come to investigate—and that no stray spark would start a fire outside.

I knew God watched over us. That knowledge kept

me going.

It hardly seemed like Christmas that December. Yet deep in our hearts, we knew that the Babe of Bethlehem had come—even for those who were turning our world upside down.

We took only what we needed for our temporary stay in the three small offices we would use. The last day of December we swept and cleaned the main house for the last time. It had never been so spotless.

In the afternoon, inspectors from the construction company came and looked through the building. They nodded approval as we handed them the keys.

"We have two requests," we said. "Will you ask your workers, please, to use the back gate? And may we continue to harvest vegetables from the garden and bury our garbage there?"

The officials agreed to both requests. "We will move in tomorrow," they said, and left.

*I*t was New Year's Eve. That evening yelps of glee from the old home startled us. *Whatever can that be?* we wondered as we went to our door.

Ogling eyes met ours at every window in the house above us. New military cadets had moved in. We stepped back into our room, locked the doors, and hung sheets over the tall windows. That night we rested uneasily.

The next morning we heard a loud crash. Locks on the doors to our part of the compound broke. Youth poured down the steps to our quarters. With a stick, they poked a hole through one of the windows and pushed aside the covering. Calling vulgar names, they peered into our room.

A sudden sharp command from above halted the assault. The mob retreated.

For ten days we heard the young soldiers' noise. Often we heard glass breaking and wood splintering. Then they left as suddenly as they had come.

The day the soldiers left, Brother One went to bury garbage. He returned to tell of shocking devastation. He also told us about the angry government workers who had come to see the damage. They had seen the property as we had left it. Now they looked at the dirty shambles.

I never went up to view the destruction. Female political prisoners were brought in. They cleaned the filth-smeared walls, windows, and floors and cleared away the dirty straw on which the soldiers had slept.

When the prisoners finished cleaning, government construction workers moved in. They didn't embarrass or harass us. In fact, some of the women secretaries came to ask for help with English. They expressed shame over what had happened.

By mid-January Dorothy and I began to slow down and plan for a late Christmas.

With a fling of rare extravagance, our faithful cook laid a fire in the long-unused office fireplace. Then he went to the kitchen to prepare a Christmas dinner. He outdid himself with vegetables from the garden and two tins of food we had hoarded.

For a few peaceful hours Dorothy and I sat before the crackling fire. We ate, dreamed, and talked about our families. We thought about the weeks past which we had faced with such fear! Now we realized how wonderfully God had taken away danger. He had also given wisdom, help, strength, and health throughout the big move. How much we had to be thankful for!

That evening Teacher Ho accepted our invitation to come and share some of our goodies. Talk turned to worship and praise as we considered the wonders of our Savior's love.

What a special day!

Chapter Twenty-Eight
Testing

By the end of the first year of communist rule, the new government made radical changes. The new rules touched everyone.

People stopped coming to church. Church offerings shrank. Along with them went the income for Teacher Ho's work with women and children. I was not surprised one afternoon when she announced, "Today I went to a factory that makes small spinning machines. I think I could learn to spin." Without a hint of bitterness she continued: "The cadres encourage home industries. I believe I can support myself this way."

It hurt me to think of all Ho-Ho had done for so many people. I resented those who no longer considered her work worthwhile.

Ho-Ho went to classes at the factory to learn how to spin. A couple weeks later, workmen installed the new equipment in her guest room. I watched as she proudly surveyed her new machine. Then she sat down to demonstrate.

The machine was supposed to spin fourteen strands

at a time. Her efforts produced only two knobby threads. "With practice, I will do it right," dear Ho-Ho said with confidence.

I went down often to watch the new spinner's progress. Once I found her standing sadly beside the machine. "You try," she said.

I was sure two quick hands and strong feet could make it work. I sat down. My efforts were just as hopeless.

Ho-Ho sent the machine back to the factory to be readjusted. Six weeks later it came back. It still produced only half the normal output. Ho-Ho had a dud. She did not have money to buy another or to send this one for repair again. We felt powerless to help her.

I sometimes relieved Ho-Ho while she rested. Authorities expected her to return a full quota of thread every week. Anna came to help after selling her vegetables. But we all knew that Ho-Ho would get little income from her efforts.

A couple of months after our move from the main mission house, authorities came again. "We are short of accommodations for our government workers," said the spokesman. "Since you are leaving soon, we want to borrow these three rooms. You may live there."

He pointed at the old storage building across the tiny yard. Brother One already lived in one room at the end of the earthen-floored structure. His little cottage had been given to the construction company with the main house.

We packed up and moved. A narrow kitchen/storage room separated our room from Brother One's. Dorothy and I divided our single room with a tall wardrobe. A table and two chairs fit snugly on one side. We could just squeeze around our double bed on the other side. Our trunks provided "counter space" in the tiny kitchen. We shared Teacher Ho's washroom and toilet below.

Cramped living made it easier to get irritated. At one stressful time, I cried, "If I ever get out of here, I'll never be a missionary again!" Mercifully, the Lord did not hold me to that bitter outburst!

One warm spring day we persuaded Brother One to help us dig up the yard in front of our rooms. We wanted to make a small vegetable garden. Our new neighbors looked on with interest. Obviously, they had not seen foreigners doing manual labor before.

With excitement, I watched as seedlings appeared. The plants leafed out, blossomed, and finally set tiny beans. One day the neighbors' children broke several of the bushes as they played. The cook staked them up. I gathered some of the young beans because I didn't think they would grow bigger on the broken plants.

The next day other bushes were down. I gathered more tender beans.

That evening three young women in uniform stood at our door. "We are from the Agricultural Department," they said. "We've come to investigate a report that you are harvesting beans before they are full-grown. That would be a waste of China's natural resources. Is that true?" they asked.

I admitted my mistake, received their caution, and thanked them for their trouble. But I wasn't really thankful! Inside I fumed. I felt especially angry when I saw the mother of the children step back from the window with a smug smile.

When our callers left, my first impulse was to go rip up the whole garden. But I knew that would cause more trouble. It could even delay our exit. How I needed God's control!

Real panic broke out another day when the cook came back from burying garbage in the old garden. With trembling lips he stammered, "They're digging a night-soil pit right where we buried that hand grenade!"

The two of us stepped into the kitchen and asked for God's protection. When Brother One regained control, he returned to the garden. He pretended to gather turnips, though we already had plenty. In the garden he could watch the digging from a distance. I waited below for his return.

An hour later Brother One returned. He held an armful of well-polished turnips. A smile lit his face. "Know what?" he said.

"No. What?" I asked.

"They dug the hole right up to a few inches from the grenade. They are now preparing to cement the pit and seal all around the edges. That thing will be safe for years." He chuckled.

Day by day I was learning more of God's marvelous care for us.

Chapter Twenty-Nine

Ostracized

A few weeks later I struggled for control again. Workmen appeared at our door. They claimed they came from a munitions plant. "We're looking for saltpeter. It is used to make gunpowder," they said. "It is found in especially dirty places. We want to check here."

Thanks! I thought.

I was totally unprepared for what happened next. The spokesman plunged a small, drilling instrument into the dirt floor at my feet. Drawing it up, he touched his tongue to the tip of it. He nodded thoughtfully. Turning to the men who waited with picks and shovels, he said, "Put the furniture outside."

Dorothy and I looked on helplessly while they emptied our room.

"This won't take long. When we've finished here, we'll do up there." The man pointed with his chin toward the big house.

Brother One's words about a gun roared into my mind. Could there really have been a gun in the house? Did the missionary dispose of it under the big house?

The workmen dug the hard-packed earth of our floor nearly one foot down. They finished by bringing a few baskets of wet, yellow clay to sprinkle on the uneven earth. The men set the furniture inside and left.

Brother One had kept an eye on the workers by busying himself in the kitchen. He now came to help arrange and level our furniture.

Teacher Ho also came up to see what had happened. I told her what the foreman said about returning tomorrow to dig under the big house. When I shared my fears of what they might find there, she frowned. She stayed only long enough for us to pray together.

Early the next morning, before the workmen arrived, she came in. "I'm spending the day with you," she announced. "I will come every day until that job is done." I hugged her!

For five days of torment, Ho-Ho, Dorothy and I knitted or sewed.

The old mission home stood on huge natural rocks. They raised the building a couple feet off the ground. Workmen dragged basketful after basketful of earth from under the big house. As time passed, we realized they were not looking for saltpeter. They wanted to see if anything was hidden there. I cried with relief when they stopped work at the kitchen floor—not far from the piece of the machete.

A few days later our neighbors moved out. They "accidentally" trampled the rest of our garden. When they had gone, the officer returned to say we might return if we wished.

"If we wished"?! We would have more space and separate rooms again! That thought made cleaning up the

mess the people had left positively pleasant. Our move had obviously been ordered so they could search the grounds before we left the country.

Through those difficult days, times with our Chinese co-workers encouraged us all.

One evening in April Teacher Ho came on a special errand. She often came just to chat, pray, or play a game of Chinese checkers. This time she seemed uneasy. Finally she revealed her mission. Speaking quietly, she said, "Pastor Philip, Andrew, the elders, and I have been talking. I must ask that you two no longer come to church meetings. There's so much anti-foreign propaganda. The people have been told to stay away from any meeting if you are present." Her black eyes glistened with tears.

After that only Ho-Ho and a blind teenager were brave enough to visit us. We valued their selfless love.

One precious moment stands out. Late one Sunday morning Teacher Ho came to our door. In her good hand she carried a small plate covered with a white handkerchief.

Dorothy and I sat having our own worship time. Stepping into the room, she set the dish on the table. She sat down and lifted the cover. "This is for you," she whispered.

In the tiny dish we saw bread and wine, brought from the communion table below. "Philip asked me to bring this to you," she said. She stopped to check her emotions. "He asked me to tell you that though you may no longer meet with us, we are still one in Christ."

Three pairs of eyes welled with tears as we remembered the One who had bound us together in Himself.

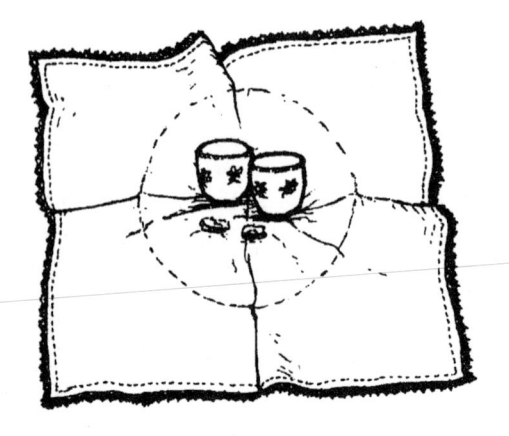

Chapter Thirty

Perfect Timing

The pink and white roses beside the house bloomed gloriously. The citrus tree outside our door poured rich fragrance into the spring air. These things should have encouraged me. Instead, I let my desire to leave China consume me. I became ill.

Dorothy brought some of the fragrant blossoms to my bedside. Teacher Ho brought the doctor.

I thought I was trusting God. But I really wanted my will, not His.

Early in May the Health Department asked me to help in an inoculation campaign. I appreciated the opportunity. I enjoyed doing it—until I became ill a second time.

"Why?" I asked bitterly.

After three days of misery, God rebuked my sin of continual complaining. *Try giving thanks for the situation instead!*

How honest can my thanks be? I wondered. Still, I tried to concentrate on what God had done for me. "Lord, I am Your child because You gave Your Son as my Savior. I am thankful for Him," I told Him. "Thank You for being with me now. Thanks for Dorothy, for dear Ho-Ho, the doctor, and medicines. Thank You for bringing Rachel and her darling baby last week. Thank You for the love and trust she has in You, even though her husband is in labor camp. Thank You for keeping him in that hard place...." The list grew.

Finally I added, with some hesitation, "Lord, I am willing to stay here as long as You want me to stay."

The next morning my fever had dropped. The nausea and vomiting had stopped. I was at peace. Thanking had worked!

Five days later Dorothy and I came back from a busy afternoon of giving shots. The gatekeeper met us. "This afternoon a policeman from the Provincial Headquarters came," he said. "You must go see him this evening."

He must have seen worry on our faces. "It's all right," he assured us. "Don't be afraid. I think your passes have come. But don't tell the police I told you!"

We raced to our rooms to clean up and to grab a bite to eat. Then we headed for the police station. We had just passed through our front gate when the gateman called, "Here he comes!"

The messenger approached us. "Your travel permits have come," he said. "You may leave as soon as there is a boat."

We hardly dared to believe our ears. We asked the

policeman go with us to Teacher Ho's room and repeat his message to her.

"It is true," he told her. "Their exit permits have been granted. All they need to do is put a three-day announcement in the paper."

"What about guarantors?" Ho-Ho asked.

"That will not be necessary for them," he replied.

We thanked him and watched him turn away. With tears, we turned to Teacher Ho. "I saw the policeman this afternoon," she told us. "But he did not reveal his mission to me."

Dear *Saint* Ho-Ho rejoiced with us as we praised and prayed together.

Months later, in America, I learned that my home church in Indianapolis had an all-night prayer meeting to ask God for my release from China. As far as we could tell, that night of prayer was the same day I submitted to God's will and used my thanksgiving key in West China.

Chapter Thirty-One

Help With Our Packing?

Ten police cadets stood at our door. We had just begun our final sorting and packing. One young man stepped forward and smiled politely. "We've come to visit," he said.

We welcomed them and brought drinking water. "We hear you're going to leave China," they said, making casual conversation.

We nodded. I wondered if they hoped for a final English lesson.

"Why are you leaving?" they continued. "Don't you love China?"

We searched for honest answers that would not cause trouble. Small talk finally became awkward silences. Then one young man asked, "Are you all packed?"

"No, we were just getting ready to do that now," we said. We hoped our words would get them to leave.

Instead, our visitors responded: "Oh, that's all right. Never mind us; go right ahead."

When the young men did not budge, we realized

they had been sent to oversee our packing. "We're in no hurry," we told them. "We are happy to chat."

Silence. Then the leader urged us to get to our work.

All day long, shift after shift of young cadets came and went. They examined everything we put in our trunks. At first they watched from the doorway. Step by step they came farther and farther into our rooms. They felt each piece of bedding, linen, and clothing as we folded it. Leafing through our books, they asked if we had maps or photos. They discussed with each other anything they questioned.

One brash young man lifted my typewriter onto the table. Opening it, he told me to roll in a sheet of paper. He carefully pecked out, "I l-o-v-e y-o-u." Pleased with himself, he looked up for my approval.

"You type very well," I said.

Closing the machine, he said, "You will not be allowed to take this." He took it to the room where they put the things we could not take. We did not challenge their decisions.

They seemed to make us leave behind the things they liked. The young typist confirmed our suspicion later in the afternoon. He retrieved the typewriter and returned it to me. "You may take this with you," he said sheepishly and disappeared. Elbow punching broke out among his fellows as he left.

The cadets examined our things less carefully after that. In fact, now they urged us to finish quickly.

*P*acking took longer than we expected. This was not only because of the surveillance. The authorities required detailed lists of the contents of each trunk. As we traveled, those lists would be checked against the items in our luggage again and again.

The sun was setting by the time we finished. A senior officer arrived. With a flourish, he fixed his seal to strips of rice paper pasted across the tops of our trunks. They also sealed the latches and padlocks. Broad strips of paper also sealed the room where the men had put the things to leave behind.

After the police left, Dorothy and I attacked the litter that remained. With a short-handled broom, I reached across one of the trunks to sweep behind it. I barely touched the lid. It popped open and the fragile seals tore!

The trunk had not closed properly when the men pasted the paper across the latch. I had mentioned it, but they said, "Never mind—it's all right." Everyone was impatient by then, so I had not argued with them. Now I regretted it. I called Dorothy, "I'll have to go to report this."

Rain lashed my face as I hurried along the dark streets. At the police station a sentry challenged, "What is your business?"

"I wish to speak with someone who visited my house today," I told him. "I have come to report a broken seal."

"Wait here!" the guard said. Then he stood at silent attention in his shelter.

Waiting in the rain, I tried to find something to be

thankful for. I watched my young "friends" inside enjoying their late meal. Hungry and thirsty, I sucked rain from my lips.

When the cadets finished eating, I explained my problem. An officer sent two reluctant men to look into the matter. Hurrying to keep up with the circle of light from their lanterns, I followed. Back at our house, the two glanced over the trunk. They locked it properly, reapplied seals, and left.

I felt so stressed out, I could not eat supper. I peeled off my muddy shoes and wet clothes, put on something dry, and slid into my sleeping bag. Beneath me I felt the rope bed. The mattress had been locked away in the sealed room. Even so, I murmured a brief thanks to my heavenly Father for the trouble-free repair of the seal.

I slipped into oblivion with one final thought: *Will departure day ever come?*

Chapter Thirty-Two
Last Preparations

The next day, Dorothy and I made four copies of each "List of Contents." We used my reclaimed typewriter.

We translated them for Teacher Ho, who made identical lists in beautiful handwritten Chinese.

That evening Brother One surprised us with a visit. He told us a passenger boat bound for Chungking was expected in four days.

We had not seen him for over a month. He had left us for another job when the authorities no longer needed him to watch us. His going relieved some of our financial problems. Making our own meals helped fill the days of waiting.

We enjoyed seeing him again, though, and appreciated his concern for our welfare.

The next morning we were summoned to help give shots at the middle school next door. It shattered our plans for a quiet Sunday.

As we entered one of the classrooms, children fled screaming. Some jumped from windows six feet above the ground. Everyone found the experience painful.

The teachers were embarrassed. The children winced at the pricks. The flashing hatred in eyes that once danced to see us stung me. Months of brain-washing had brought hurtful changes.

We wondered how we could be ready to leave the next day if they asked us to help again. No one came to call us. Instead, we visited provincial, district and local offices to "sign out" and turn in property deeds and keys.

At the Land Registration Office, the official behind an imposing desk received us in a businesslike manner. Explaining our errand, Dorothy laid the deeds to mission property on his desk.

He did not reach for the papers. "The transfer of land in China is a very serious matter, you know," he said. "Ordinarily we could not receive these. But since you are leaving our country, we will hold them until your return."

Our last trip was to collect our travel and exit permits at Provincial Police Headquarters. To our great surprise, we saw Walter Jespersen and Edith Jackson there. Like us, they were getting ready to leave China. They had arrived four days before but had not been allowed to visit or send word to us.

In the few seconds we had together, we learned we would travel together. What relief! We were especially glad to have a man in our travel party!

When the officer completed and stamped our documents, he handed them to us. He showed us to the door politely and expressed regret at our going. Something in his manner made me wonder if he was a brother in Christ.

Chapter Thirty-Three

Caught with Contraband

Our last evening in Luhsien, Teacher Ho came to see that we had everything ready. We were just finishing up.

I picked up the large handbag I had for the journey. I had not used it in years. Opening it, I found six dimes and a U.S. two-dollar bill. I had completely forgotten them!

Ho-Ho stared at the bill. "Well!" she exclaimed, "You will have to get rid of *that* before morning. You should have turned it in months ago."

"I know," I said soberly. "I'll burn it in the morning."

Teacher Ho left about midnight. Slipping my hand into hers, I gave it a squeeze. With a kiss I whispered in her ear, "I wish I could take you with me."

Tears came to Ho-Ho's eyes. She shook her head. Turning, she went down the steps.

The next morning, I pushed back the predawn darkness with my small flashlight. As I dressed, I saw the familiar figures of Teacher Ho, Pastor Philip, Andrew, and Anna moving around the small charcoal stoves behind Teacher Ho's room. I wondered how early they had begun making breakfast. They had invited Dorothy and me to a good-bye meal at seven thirty.

My throat tightened at the thought of leaving. *I'll see them in Heaven, but will I ever see them down here again?*

I stood watching for a few moments. Then I lit the lamp and picked up my devotional book, *Daily Light on the Daily Path*, and turned to May 30. The last words in that morning's portion seized my attention. "The Lord will be your everlasting light, and your God will be your glory" (Is. 60:19).

Tears came as I pondered God's promise. I thought about the future we all faced. We had passed through dangerous times together. More would follow.

I knew the promise was as true for those staying as for those of us leaving. But our friends would probably experience greater trials.

Shuffling feet on the path outside told me someone was coming. I went to the window. Brother One stood there looking up. He held a small lighted bundle of sticks in one hand. "Something for your breakfast," he called. He held up a small parcel in his other hand.

I went outside to receive the warm bag. It had been made from a copy sheet of some child's school book. I peeked inside at warm sweet rolls. "Oh, thank you, Brother One," I said, bowing.

Turning to leave, he said, "I must go to the market now. I'll return at nine o'clock to rope up your trunks and take them to the boat."

Going back to my room, I prayed for the young man. *Lord, let him live in your light and seek to glorify You.*

Dorothy and I each munched on a roll as we did up our hand luggage. We were almost done packing when the call came for breakfast.

Spread on Teacher Ho's table lay a feast of love. We spent a comfortable, relaxed hour there. The Lord was very near as we encouraged one another with promises from His Word. I shared my early-morning gem.

When time came to go, the two men told us they would not go to the wharf with us. "It seems wiser," they said.

"But we'll go with you," Ho-Ho and Anna promised.

Our hearts were tight with the pain of parting. Hurrying outside, we found Brother One and his friends, ready to rope up our luggage. They had just begun when twelve soldiers burst into the courtyard. "Open those trunks!" one of the soldiers commanded.

With quaking hearts, we replied, "Oh, but we can't do that! The police sealed them three days ago." We pointed to the official red stamps on the paper seals.

"Open them!" the leader of the band shouted.

Trying to explain only nettled the man. Angry that we refused to obey, the soldiers slit the seals with their bayonets. "Now," the leader commanded, "unlock them!"

Dorothy and I each opened a trunk. The soldiers rummaged through the contents. When they had shaken out and tossed every item from the two trunks onto the ground, they turned to another. "Open that one!" they snapped, pointing to my second trunk.

"Sir, I cannot do that until I have repacked this one," I protested, "or things will get mixed up. Then our 'contents lists' will be wrong."

Impatiently, two men lent a hand. The lid would not close. While the agitated soldiers watched, I lifted the contents from the trunk. Carefully refolding each item, I repacked it and closed the lid. The search through the second trunk was cursory.

During that tense hour I remembered the money I had found. While the soldiers finished Dorothy's trunks, I excused myself and went up to my room. Snatching up the two-dollar bill, I stuffed it into my dress.

Then I heard footsteps on the stairs. Quickly, I looked for a crack where I could drop the dimes. Too late! The bold soldiers came right into my room.

"What are you doing?" they asked suspiciously.

"A little last-minute packing," I replied. "Our boat is due soon."

The soldiers looked about the room and spotted the coins on my desk. "What are those?" they demanded.

"A little American money." I answered as casually as my pounding heart would allow.

"How much is it worth in our money?" they wanted to know.

After rapid calculation, I answered, "Several hundred yuan."

"Didn't you know it's against the law to have American money?" They spat the words at me.

Other "comrades" now crowded in. Dorothy followed them into the room.

"It's the money," I said quietly.

With a charge against me now, the soldiers whooped, "To the police station with you!"

Chapter Thirty-Four

At the Police Station

*A*n angry soldier swept his arm across my desk, scattering everything. I grabbed at my bag and scrambled to the floor for my exit permit, passport, and travel money. I was reaching for my Bible, when a second command, "Go!" came.

We gathered up what we could, and stumbled out the door and down the steps. The soldiers pressed close behind us. Brother One and the carriers had already gone with our trunks. When the soldiers saw that, they swore. Obviously they had plans for them.

Teacher Ho and Anna stood in their doorway, silent. I glanced their way without a word or look that could implicate them and left the old compound.

Outside, the curious had gathered to see what was happening to the foreigners. The soldiers flourished their weapons and prodded us along the street. At the intersection to a local police station, I turned. A bayonet jabbed my back. "Where do you think you're going?" someone yelled.

"To the police station," I replied.

"Not this one. You're going to Provincial Headquarters uptown."

As we turned back onto the main street, I breathed a sign of relief. We had received our travel documents at Provincial Headquarters the evening before. The officials there were not boys. I thought of the courteous officer. *Lord*, I prayed, *please send Your angel before us!*

We created quite a scene with twelve soldiers and bayonets at our backs! But by the end of our forced march through the city we scarcely drew a glance. Only two teen-aged soldiers still followed us. Their guns were now shouldered.

Our young captors seemed unable to explain our presence to the guard outside police headquarters. They released us to him and hurried away. The guard led us to the building we had visited the previous day. The courteous officer we had met before seemed surprised to see us. "What brings you back?" he asked.

I explained about the dimes.

"How much money have you?" was his next question.

I laid six coins on his desk. Looking at his watch, he spoke, "Your boat leaves soon, doesn't it?"

"That's correct," I replied.

"You will need to write a confession," he said. He pushed a sheet of paper and writing equipment toward me.

"Though I write a little Chinese character, I am not good enough to compose such a document," I responded.

The officer got up from his desk. "Wait here!" he said and left the room.

It seemed one of the longest waits of my life. I wondered if my exit permit would be canceled. In the middle of torturing thoughts, however, I found a place where my "thanksgiving key" fit. *Thank You, Lord, for a quiet room where no one is shouting at me.*

The officer returned thirty-five minutes later. He held a carefully written legal paper. "Sign here, then you may go," he said.

I hesitated, wondering if I had heard correctly. "Sign here," he repeated. He pointed to a space at the lower left corner.

Without reading my confession, I signed it!

"That is all," he said quietly.

Close to tears, I thanked him simply. Then I added, "God bless you, sir."

Again with a slight nod, the man turned and escorted us to the door. Surely he was God's angel!

Silently thankful, Dorothy and I left the building. Dorothy had a final errand at the post office. I went directly to the inn to find our fellow-missionary travelers. I barely acknowledged their greeting or the babble of their excited children. Instead, I begged to go to their sleeping quarters. Alone at last, I burst into tears.

Chapter Thirty-Five

Good-bye to Luhsien

*M*inutes later I heard Teacher Ho's voice. Entering the room, she sat down on the bed beside me. She laid her hand gently on my convulsing shoulder. "What happened this morning?" she asked.

Between sobs I told her about the sixty cents.

"I told you to get rid of that money," she scolded.

"Yes, I know. But I forgot to do it before breakfast." Then I added, "How did you get here?"

"I waited until the furor died down. Then I left the compound," she said. "I took the west road that goes outside the wall through the country. I came back around through east gate. Anna came another way. She's outside. We had to know what happened."

Our friends called from the outer room, "We hear the boat whistle! That means we can buy our tickets."

Teacher Ho got up. "By the way, what about the two-dollar bill?"

"It's here," I said, touching the front of my dress. "I'll throw it into the river when we get going."

"What!" she exclaimed. "You still have that bill?

Don't you know you'll be searched when you go on the boat? Give it to me!"

I handed Ho-Ho the crumpled bill. As she left the room, I noticed that she limped more than usual.

At the wharf, a long flight of temporary wooden steps stretched to the shallow river. As I picked my way down them, I suddenly realized Ho-Ho was at my elbow. "Ho-Ho," I said, "did you get rid of it?"

She nodded.

"Did you burn it?"

She shook her head.

"You didn't give it to anyone?

Again she shook her head no.

"What *did* you do with it?" I asked.

She showed me the tip of her tongue. The last tiny piece of the two-dollar bill covered it.

"Oh, but it couldn't have tasted good!" I exclaimed.

She shook her head vigorously. "No, it wasn't a very tasty snack."

Other passengers crowded to get past us on the narrow steps. "Thank you, thank you, beloved teacher," I whispered, and turned away.

Teacher Ho limped back up the steps to join Anna and Brother One on the bank. We boarded the boat and found the luggage Brother One had put in our cabins. Then we returned to stand by the rail and wave goodbye.

I saw Teacher Ho turn to Brother One. He pivoted and disappeared into the crowd. Reappearing shortly, he brought two paper bags to the wharf. "Teacher Ho thought the children might get hungry before next meal time," he called. He left the bags with the steward.

Inside them we found fourteen sweet moon-cakes. The loving, sacrificial gift touched us deeply. I was glad to have been included among "the children."

The loyal three stayed on the riverbank until we lifted anchor about 2:30 p.m. We responded to their flutter of large handkerchiefs until a bend in the river separated us from view.

One day I shall look for the welcoming flutter of handkerchiefs on another shore. At least Teacher Ho has already gone on ahead. Ron and Gwen Roberts, my first senior workers at Luhsien, returned as tourists to West Sichuan in 1980. They learned she had been struck by a moving truck about a year before. She was killed instantly.

Dear Ho-Ho—"with Christ, which is far better."

Chapter Thirty-Six

Road to Freedom

The steamer carried us swiftly away, running with the current.

The parting still weighed on my heart. But traveling with friends we had not seen for nearly two years lifted my spirits. We forgot time as we exchanged stories about what had happened to us.

Twenty-four hours after leaving Luhsien we reached Chungking. There we had to finish exit formalities and travel arrangements. The hours of questioning seemed endless. At the same time, being with friends and knowing we were on our way to freedom encouraged us.

After eighteen days at Chungking, authorities let us travel on. We bought passage on a small freighter. It was shallow enough to travel the treacherous Yangtze Gorge rapids in low-water season.

Six of us faced the journey in the windowless hold of the overloaded boat. A single dim light held back the darkness. By boarding early, we found a place near one of the loading hatches. There an occasional breeze from outside freshened the dank air.

The interrogations had emotionally and physically drained us. We hardly minded when people stumbled over or around us. Carriers came to load coal. Other passengers came to share our quarters.

Helen Jespersen and her four children found quarters above. To be sure we did not lose our place, we did not go see them often. We slept much of that two-and-a-half-day trip. That meant we missed most of the famous gorges.

From our water-level hatch we could see mountains rearing straight up from surging rapids. But the view was marred by the sight of corpses churning in the rapids. Finally the choked river burst from its rocky confines onto a broad plain.

*E*ventually the freighter carried us to a sprawling city. We expected to transfer to a passenger boat. None of us suspected what misery awaited us!

Since we needed "special handling," we were last off the boat. They ferried us to the river's edge. There we waited with a group of fourteen nuns and a priest until all baggage had come ashore.

That accomplished, authorities handed us over to an evil innkeeper. The man refused to let us go outside the filthy inn for any reason. We were virtually prisoners. We had to depend on him for every need.

Our captors forbade us to communicate with the nuns. However, when one of the Jespersen children developed diarrhea, they slipped Walter some medicine. It probably saved the child's life.

Daily we heard boat whistles. The innkeeper insisted no space was available on them. By postponing our departure, he brought in handsome fees from twenty-six unwilling guests.

Each day we carried our clothes and bedding to the flat roof of the inn. We searched and crushed hundreds of bedbugs crowding seams and folds. I doubt the proprietor appreciated our

153

help in cutting down the hotel's bedbug population. Still, it gave us something to do.

We shall never know how long we might have stayed there if a Chinese guest at the inn had not spoken to Walter. "They have no right to keep you here," he whispered. "A steamer went out empty this morning. Another will leave tomorrow." With his finger he traced a cross on the palm of his hand and hurried on down the steps.

Prompted by that information, the men in our party demanded to go see for themselves. Reluctantly the proprietor agreed to "go again and check." He returned with tickets for all, at one-and-a-half times the regular fare. He did not let us go until sunset—after another expensive meal!

Rain was falling heavily when he shouted, "Now go! Get out!"

Leaders in our group asked for rickshaws. We needed them to take some of the elderly, crippled nuns to the wharf. When only two rickshaws came, the innkeeper insisted they take the mother of the sick child and the person carrying the six-month-old infant—me! I felt indignation and shame as we rode past the older women sloshing painfully along the darkening streets.

Chapter Thirty-Seven

Stopped at the Border!

*T*he river steamer seemed from another world. In fact, it was! The luxury ship we found at the pier had once belonged to a Dutch company. When they welcomed us aboard the spacious vessel, we found the drastic change almost bewildering. Large, clean cabins and warm water for bathing helped soothe the strain of the past days.

The next day we washed our clothes. We hung our things to dry on lines rigged by a helpful steward. The steamer decks looked like a laundry yard.

The ship had carried others from that infamous city. Some, the crew members told us, had been held for three weeks.

For two nights and a day we steamed through central China. At Hankow, the junction of the Yangtze River and the state-run southern railroad, we spent a full day.

During the grueling inspection, one of the Jespersen children, a blond five-year-old in a blue sunbonnet, climbed on top of a pile of luggage. Then she broke into song. Her choice of music was a communist propaganda song. She had learned it from cadets practicing on the badminton court at her home in West China! Soldiers and police gathered around and clapped. After that the authorities seemed less intrusive.

In the evening we boarded a comfortable train. It took us on another two-and-a-half day journey to Canton.

In Canton, travel agents (actually plain-clothes policemen) met us. They helped us to a hotel. The next morning they woke us early and hustled us back to the train station for another luggage examination.

At the end of another five hours on the train we found ourselves sweltering in a tin-roofed shed. We were only yards from China's border with Hong Kong.

In the shed, we went through our third frisk and eighth and most thorough baggage "turn out." As we gathered our scattered things, we looked longingly toward a huge British flag. It fluttered beyond the barbed-wire barrier.

The travel agents escorted the repacked luggage across the border. Meanwhile, the Jespersens, Edith, and two Swiss workers moved through the barricade. Still on the China side, I walked behind Dorothy toward the same portal to freedom. At the barricade, we would surrender our travel passes and exit permits.

When we reached the gate Dorothy frantically searched for her papers. They *had* been in her bag! We heard one of the guards say, "You must go back."

Every ounce of energy drained from me.

Dorothy could not have boarded the train in Canton nor come into the examination shed without a pass. Where could it have gone?

Beyond the barrier, Walter heard and saw the growing commotion. He stepped back to the gate. As Dorothy explained her problem to him, a guard broke in. "She must go back to Chungking," he said sternly.

"Would you allow her to go and see if the papers are in her baggage that has gone ahead?" Walter asked. "It's just over there." He pointed to the pile of jumbled boxes and trunks on the Hong Kong side.

"No!" came the curt reply.

"If I cross back to China's side and stand in her place," asked Walter, "would you let her go with the travel agent to look for it?"

To this the border guards agreed.

I waited on China's soil, clutching my all-important papers securely. I prayed Dorothy would quickly find hers and thanked the Lord for a family man who unselfishly volunteered to stand in for a single co-worker.

Dorothy returned waving the precious papers. She had put them in another bag. Once she handed the permits to the unsmiling guard, she and Walter turned toward the border. Numb with fear, I surrendered my travel pass and exit permit and walked through the small gate in the barbed-wire barrier.

All I wanted was to get far away from the border. I resisted a strong impulse to run up the footpath that led away from that gate.

Hong Kong police in spotless uniforms and gleaming boots stepped forward. "This way, Teachers," they directed politely. They pointed to the immigration building below the huge "Union Jack." The rippling flag quivered in the breeze. My heart also quivered as tears welled in my eyes.

The solemn faces of officers relaxed into smiles. They had witnessed the exchanges at the border. "You can be glad you found your papers," one of them told Dorothy. "We've recently seen two others sent back from that gate. They have not returned."

I stared back at the narrow gate we had just passed through and shuddered.

"It's all right. You're safe now," comforted an observant officer. "You can't be taken back from here."

*I*nside Immigration, officials quickly examined and stamped our passports. When they were done, they hustled us off to the train that waited for us. Leaning from open windows, passengers cheered as the two of us climbed aboard.

We had no sooner found our seats than a trembling voice started to sing. It was the Doxology. "Praise God from whom all blessings flow," in several languages, spread from car to car.

Praise God who had kept me safe—and kept me true to my promise made so many years ago.

The Adventurer Series

God's Adventurer

Huson Taylor was still a teenager when God told him to go to China. Alone, broke and even critically ill, he hung on to that goal, and to God who was sending him. But would God be enough? In inland China, Hudson had lots of chances to find out! There is plenty of danger, adventure and action in this true story of a man who dared to risk all on God.

The Promise

One disapppointing night, Mary makes a promise to God. Little does she know it will carry her half way around the world and throw her into the hands of the communists! Mary's promise takes her to China in 1947, just two years before the communist takeover. As her life gets more and more restricted, Mary struggles to stay true to her promise—and to be thankful in everything. But it is this "thanksgiving key" that will open the door to freedom.